D0065192

FROM
MIND
TO
MARKET

FROM MIND TO MARKET

REINVENTING THE RETAIL SUPPLY CHAIN

ROGER D. BLACKWELL

HarperBusiness
A Division of HarperCollinsPublishers

HarperCollins books may be purchased for educational, business, or sales promotional use. For information please write: Special Markets Department, HarperCollins Publishers, Inc., 10 East 53rd Street, New York, NY 10022.

FIRST EDITION

Designed by Joseph Rutt

Library of Congress Cataloging-in-Publication Data

Blackwell, Roger D.
   From mind to market : reinventing the retail supply chain / by Roger D. Blackwell. — 1st ed.
      p.   cm.
   Includes index.
   ISBN 0-88730-833-3
   1. Relationship marketing. 2. Consumers' preferences. 3. Retail trade.   I. Title.
HF5415.55.B58   1997
658.8'7—dc21   97-25822

97 98 99 00 01 ❖/RRD 10 9 8 7 6 5 4 3 2 1

This book is dedicated to Kristina Stephan Blackwell

- *my partner*
- *my reason*
- *my love*

—Roger D. Blackwell

Contents

ACKNOWLEDGMENTS

It has been said that a journey of a thousand miles begins with a single step, but the preparation of this book reversed that process. It began with 1,000 pages of manuscript and, with the help of many guides and fellow travelers, ended with the book you see today. It is a book that I hope you will find not only beneficial and provocative, but also a delight to read.

I am fortunate to have good friends with the experience and wisdom to examine critically the concepts and the willingness to read the first draft and make valuable suggestions. Some of these include Dr. David Kollat, who started his career as a professor but redirected it toward consulting at Management Horizons and, later, operations and strategy as a senior executive at The Limited. Another reviewer of the first draft was Stig Kry, chairman emeritus of the highly respected consulting firm Kurt Salmon Associates. I benefited greatly from other executives who read most or all of the manuscript in various stages of revision. These include Jack Shewmaker, former CEO of Wal-Mart; Don Boyce, chairman of Idex Corporation; Tom Moser of KPMG-Peat Marwick; and Jack Kahl, CEO of Manco, who acted as far more than a source of advice and encouragement, but also as a trusted friend.

As you read about each company described in the following pages, I hope you will share my gratitude to the management and staff of the companies who helped me collect materials for the book. Special thanks for going the "extra mile" are due to Kinko's, JCPenney, Applied Industrial Technology, Banc One, Consolidated Stores, Avon, Service Corporation International, PETsMART, Ford, American Airlines, Cardinal Health, Newell, Harry Rosen, Longaberger Baskets, and Enron. While many other companies assisted us as well, associates of these companies endured repeated phone calls from me and my staff and often spent hours searching for facts that I needed. I deeply appreciate their help. I also want to thank Ed Razek, senior VP for marketing at The Limited for his help. And of course, special gratitude goes to Leslie Wexner, chairman of The Limited, Intimate Brands, and Abercombie & Fitch, for writing the foreword. I believe that, next to Sam Walton, Leslie Wexner has probably shaped retailing in the 20th century more than any other individual. I am honored that after reading chapters of the first draft, Leslie Wexner was willing to lend his name and thoughts to this project.

If you find this book fun to read, much of the credit should go to Laureen Connelly Rowland, editor at HarperBusiness, who provided enormous vision and focus for the book. I am also appreciative to Kirsten Sandberg, who started the book on its journey and cemented my relationship with HarperBusiness.

The production of the book was coordinated at many points by Kelley Hughes, office manager at Blackwell Associates, Inc., keeper of my calendar and ultimate support system. I would also like to thank the entire Blackwell Associates team of Sandy Proper; Andrea Ravagnani, for her research assistance; and John Welday, for his technical support. I am also indebted to my colleagues at the Ohio State University, especially the marketing faculty where I teach, and the Supply Chain Management Group, for their research on topics essential to my analysis of supply chains.

Many authors give credit to their parents, but in my case it is genuine. My father's nearly 50 years as a business school teacher and professor have inspired me, and my mother's lifetime in retailing provided me with a firsthand understanding of retailing and consumer behavior that started in my childhood. Trudy and Alfred Stephan have also helped us with many of the practical aspects of life during the time my wife, Tina, and I have written this book. Their time and support have allowed us to end this process with sanity.

The person who deserves the most credit, however, is Tina. She has truly been a coauthor, cutting the original manuscript to half the size, suggesting ideas and examples, and participating in the writing of every word of the final manuscript. Without her help and encouragement, and 18-hour workdays, I doubt that this book would have made it from our minds to market.

FOREWORD

Business and life are all about changing and adapting. Change keeps us strong. Clearly, businesses must constantly search for structures that encourage the flow of creative energy. That has always been our goal at The Limited, and it is the topic Roger Blackwell addresses in his new book, *From Mind to Market*.

Today more than ever, businesses of all types must dedicate themselves to continual learning. Not only do we need to learn as organizations, but we need to provide a learning environment for our associates. When we enrich individuals, we transform workplaces into "think places" that foster the creativity and knowledge needed to become mind-to-market leaders.

Dr. Blackwell has captured well many of the themes that underlie our evolution at The Limited. But the principles and methods he describes can be used by any business to survive and thrive in the new century.

In this important book, Dr. Blackwell addresses a number of pressing questions including: How can we expand the opportunities for business in the 21st century? Can we develop new kinds of business organizations that will better enable us to invent, nurture, and grow exciting concepts? Can our businesses draw and learn from each other to maximize performance? Do we have the leanness and agility to maintain and encourage our entrepreneurial energy? Dr. Blackwell answers these and other questions in his book, which, ultimately, will help readers better serve that ultimate master—the customer.

Some firms do things right, and some firms do the right things. But the best firms figure out how to do the right things right. *From Mind to Market* tells you how to be one of those.

—*Leslie H. Wexner, chairman, The Limited, Inc.*

Introduction

For more than 30 years, I've been fielding questions about the business world of tomorrow from CEOs and students alike: "How can you tell which companies will be around for the long haul—to invest in or work for?" they ask. Or: "How can I best grow my firm?" And this: "What's a good business to get into?"

In my dual roles as professor of marketing at the Ohio State University and as marketing-strategy consultant for a diverse group of *Fortune* 500 clients, I've long been identifying consumer trends that point to untapped niches and new growth opportunities for consumer and industrial firms. And, for years, as I've traveled the globe speaking to executives and their sales forces about the business and retail landscape of tomorrow, I've been thrust into the role of making forecasts. Despite some ups and downs, during the last three decades, the picture generally has been rosy.

But as we approach the new millennium, the American gravy train has slowed. What was once a competitive environment in which many good players could—and did—win is evolving into one best characterized as "hypercompetitive." This new reality is the result of the convergence of a number of forces—among them, the emergence of the harried, time-pressured consumer; overbuilt retail space; a declining middle class; and the reality of the global marketplace—that are rightly causing business owners, suppliers, manufacturers, wholesalers, employers and employees, and Jane and Joe Q. Public anxiety. These and other factors are putting the squeeze on today's corporations as well as ma-and-pa businesses. Looking into the crystal ball of tomorrow, I would have to forecast a future in which excellence will be the minimal requirement to stay in the game.

We've entered what I call "an era of compression." With falling birth rates and shrinking family size, there will be fewer new consumers to buy goods and services; at the same time, veteran shoppers are growing weary of the "hunt" and spending less time at it than in the past. What's more, with corporate downsizing and increased automation, our economy will be run by a smaller workforce. As a result, the American economy is unlikely to ever again experience the double-digit growth of post-depression/post–World War II 1950s and '60s, or the expansion of the '70s and '80s that was fueled largely by women's entrance into the paid workforce. And don't bet the ranch on Jack Kemp's forecast of a coming economic boom.

Looking at the business environment of today, I'd say that, overall, 20 percent of today's companies are doing most things right; another 30 percent are stumbling along; and the other 50 percent are destined to fold their tents during the 21st century.

But not all is doom and gloom. In fact, quite the opposite is true for firms that understand the changing marketplace and can adapt to it. Sound strategies do exist for success in the 21st century. No matter what your product or service—whether you make widgets, sell everlasting flower arrangements, or offer shiatsu massage—the winners of tomorrow will be united by a common ability: *the ability to penetrate the mind of the consumer*. I will go so far as to say that this approach will no longer be optional—one of those "I'm-a-progressive-marketer" type frills; it will be mandatory. In fact, those who listen to their customers and in turn create positive images and associations will occupy a spot in that most valuable of all spaces—the gray matter inside the customer's head.

Among companies of all types and sizes, the key to future growth will come from knowing:

- How to overcome the problem of too many businesses chasing too few customers.

- How to know what consumers will want to buy in the future.

- How retailers can use multiple channels to reach new consumers.

- How improved logistics can cut costs and increase customer satisfaction.

My book, *From Mind to Market*, examines a number of forward-thinking and -acting companies—what I call "mind-to-market" leaders—and will enable readers to develop a competitive edge and in some cases establish marketplace dominance in the coming era of compression. It provides companies of any type, in any industry, with guidelines for shaking up their own supply chains. In the traditional supply chain, retailers sell products that manufacturers conceive and wholesalers supply. It is a linear, left-to-right progression in which the consumer stands passively at the receiving end of the chain. Rather than building and operating their supply chain from manufacturer to market, the best firms in the next century will form their supply chains from mind (of the consumer) to market, creating chains based on consumers' needs, wants, problems, and lifestyles. Those who lead these reconstituted supply chains (which I use interchangeably with "demand chains") are already several generations evolved from the traditional business-school model of supply-chain management.

In the future, businesses will need to reinvent themselves and their demand chains based on marketing—yes, *marketing*. Though the term may sound familiar, in fact, marketing has been largely ignored by retailers and others in favor of selling. (*Selling* is getting rid of what you have, while *marketing* is having what you can get rid of.) A genuine and dedicated marketing approach revolutionizes the marketplace by fully integrating the consumer within the supply chain to create exactly what he or she wants and needs.

Consumers are already vitally connected to the retail experience—by shopping at stores, in catalogs, and on the Internet—making the retailer as a rule the best point on the chain to collect consumer data. But as businesses of all types become consumer-based, *all* companies will need to have some mechanisms in place for consumers to express their thoughts and feelings, as well as systems to transform those ideas into products and bring them quickly to market.

This consumer-driven realignment is already occurring at our nation's fast-growing visionary companies. After I spoke at one of Wal-Mart's famous Saturday-morning meetings last year in Bentonville, Arkansas, one of the executives commented: "We don't *sell* stuff, we buy stuff for consumers." While it would be easy to dismiss this distinction as mere semantics, in fact, this self-definition—not as a retailer but as "a purchasing agent for consumers"—represents a key tenet in Wal-Mart's marketing philosophy. Without making similar changes, perhaps only a monopoly concessionaire selling soft drinks and hamburgers in a remote national park would be able to survive by using the outmoded "take-it-or-leave-it" approach to sales.

Whether this consumer-based tilt in corporate America is the result of demand-chain management or the driver toward it, the outlook on the business horizon is the same. Demand-chain management will emerge as a central business practice of tomorrow, in which players start the cycle by delving into the mind of the consumer and end it by delivering this consumer-conceived product into his or her hands. The chain is circular rather than linear; and consumer input will be solicited throughout. "Speed to market" is the description I give when this process occurs quickly and seamlessly. Once customers get used to seeing what they want on the shelves when they want it, they'll never go back to the old way. It's analogous to the leap letter writers make when introduced to on-line services. Once they've tried instantaneous communication, old-fashioned "snail mail" forever after seems painfully slow.

Readers might argue that plumbing the mind of the consumer is hardly a new idea—the best merchants have been picking customers' minds since the days Marshall Field asked women whether they preferred buttoned or string-tied corsets. But we who analyze consumer behavior are pushing the envelope of consumer exploration even further by studying not only why people buy but how they *consume*. For instance, we'd like to know not only what makes someone pick up one brand of paper towels over another but how she takes the product home, opens and disposes of the plastic overwrap, how often she uses the towels, how many sheets she tears off at a time, and what she uses them for.

Mind-to-market concepts can be applied in many other contexts, such as the nonprofit arena. For instance, boards of directors of local United Ways might want to know the minds of their donors and communities better. Administrators of colleges, universities, and government agencies could adapt these principles and techniques to better understand their "clients." Focusing on supply chains will also help savvy investors spot the Wal-Marts of the future before everyone else does. By learning how to identify the characteristics of mind-to-market leaders in real-life companies, you can identify which firms are poised to grow in the future. Great growth firms—even ones as spectacular as Intel, Disney, Microsoft, and Berkshire Hathaway—must eventually slow their growth or even decline. The trick is to anticipate the time they will slow their growth (leading to a tumble in their price/earnings ratio) about six months before financial analysts recognize what's happening.

My goal with *From Mind to Market* is to take readers through the demand-chain process, from beginning to end, allowing individuals to pull out the topics most helpful to them in preparing for the business battles of the next century. While no one firm featured in this book is perfect, I believe we can all learn from their successes by examining their strengths.

Even though I'm as at home in the boardroom as in the classroom, I consider myself first and foremost a teacher. Having taught at Ohio State since 1965, I've had the pleasure and responsibility of guiding the minds of nearly 60,000 students. Their energy, interests, talents, and questions have often led me in new directions. And while it's often mistakenly assumed that anyone working in academia is stuck in some ivory tower, the reality is that by watching and listening to students—the target consumers of the 21st century—I'm privy to the trends of tomorrow *today*.

With this book, I invite readers to explore the mind-to-market concepts that will revolutionize how businesses operate and compete in the next century. Then take them with you and use the concepts to create success in your own endeavors.

one

CONSUMER-DRIVEN DEMAND CHAINS

"Ideas are like rabbits. You get a couple and learn how to
handle them, and pretty soon you have a dozen."
—JOHN STEINBECK

SHAKING UP SUPPLY CHAINS

Wal-Mart versus Kmart. Kodak versus Fuji. Motorola versus Texas
Instruments. In the past, retailers fought wars against other retailers, while manufacturers and wholesalers likewise duked it out with
their own kind. Each entity was strong enough to take on its own
competitors. Whether these companies survived and flourished or
languished and folded was largely a result of how they performed in
relation to their peers.

In the new millennium, the rules of battle will be rewritten. No
retailer, manufacturer, or wholesaler will be strong enough to win
on its own. Great firms will fight the war for dominance in the marketplace not against individual competitors in their field but forti-
fied by alliances with wholesalers, manufacturers, and suppliers all
along the supply chain. In essence, competitive dominance will be

achieved by an entire supply chain, with battles fought supply chain versus supply chain.

Traditional supply chains begin at the point of manufacture and end with the sale to Jane or Joe Q. Public. They encompass all of the organizations and functions necessary to complete the flow of goods to the market, as shown in Figure 1.1. The manufacturers—ironically, the firms most removed from the consumer market—have traditionally dictated what consumers could buy from retailers. The focus of the supply chain has been the product that manufacturers produce. Often as not, these products were derived not from demonstrated need or consumer preference but from the manufacturer's historic strengths, resources, and best instincts.

Stellar, visionary firms are already reconfiguring the battlefield with a stronger "stealth" weapon—a newfangled supply chain tailored for the coming age of compression in the business world. This new chain caters and responds to consumer desire, which stands at both the beginning and end point of the chain.

This is the *demand* chain, which gets its name from serving that ultimate master—the mother of all transactions in the world of business—that is, the consumer.

As Figure 1.2 shows, a demand chain represents a circular process that flows from the mind of the consumer to the market. Demand chains consist of nonlinear, boundary-spanning organizations.

Figure 1.1   Traditional Supply Chain

Manufacturer ⟶ Wholesaler ⟶ Retailer ⟶ Consumer

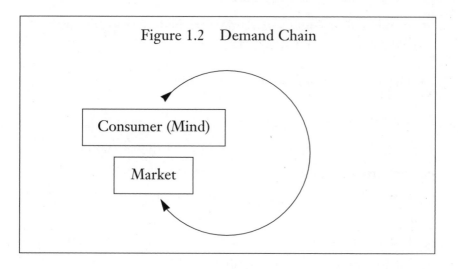

Figure 1.2   Demand Chain

TAKING THE REINS OF THE DEMAND CHAIN

Among today's cutting-edge demand chains, the players are the same as in the traditional supply chain, but the rules of the game have changed. The roles and responsibilities of each demand chain member are not based on historical strengths or traditional roles. Rather, responsibilities are assumed by the demand chain as a whole. The firm best able to complete a role does so—even if it means breaking the mold. Unlike traditional supply chains, the roles and responsibilities of players within the demand chain are fluid, dynamic, and customer-focused.

The best demand-chain players will use knowledge and innovative capability rather than size or position to gain a competitive edge. Companies jockeying for the position of demand chain leader must be able to:

- Assimilate knowledge about consumers and the market.

- Communicate that knowledge with other demand chain members and facilitate its implementation.

- Adopt and promote a marketing orientation throughout the organization and demand chain.

- Organize goals for the demand chain.

The movement toward the aforementioned changes is already well under way. Manufacturers dominated the supply chain for a century, from the end of the Civil War to the mid-1960s, when the great retailers began to emerge as major players. Over the last 30 years, supply chains have been undergoing a gradual metamorphosis, being increasingly controlled by players other than manufacturers. In today's market, the dominant retailer Wal-Mart, the brand distributor Nike, and Cardinal Health, the $8.9-billion drug wholesaler, are but a few examples. From their powerful berths in the world of commerce, these innovative firms are able to call the shots about product attributes, such as packaging and pricing; they've even extended their authority into the areas of advertising, transportation, and storage. In the cases of the three companies mentioned, the supply chains they command have achieved competitive superiority in such attributes as price, efficiency, speed to market, and accuracy of product delivery.

In the next century, companies will have to do not only what today's visionary companies are doing—by taking command of supply chains—but they'll have to evolve them into demand chains. Tapping the minds of consumers and understanding what they want to buy, how and why they buy, and how their lifestyles are changing represent the first step. Demand-chain leaders then use knowledge of consumer wants to develop products people will snap up. In a demand chain, products don't necessarily originate from manufacturers: They can be developed at any point and by any player in the chain.

Manco, the Westlake, Ohio, distributor of tapes, weather stripping, and mailing supplies, is an example of a company that started out as a wholesaler but stepped outside the traditional boundaries of that role and established itself as a mind-to-market leader. By implementing a number of rather unconventional strategies, Manco was able to both redefine and transcend its role as a wholesaler while establishing a dominant position in its demand chain. Among other things, it developed new products at the behest of its customers. At the same time, the company developed techniques to help its customers control their inventories, helping to cement long-term relationships.

AND A DUCK SHALL LEAD THEM

With projected sales of $170 million in 1997, Manco is hardly a "big boy" in the world of commerce. Nevertheless, the company stands as one of America's exemplars in mind-to-market management. How could the company that distributes a humble product like *duct tape*—which neither manufactures nor retails the stuff—have so much to teach the rest of us?

The secret lies in the command Manco has over its demand chain, a position anchored in its "customer-is-king" orientation. Armed with an unquenchable thirst for knowledge and an irrepressible entrepreneurial spirit, Manco's vibrant chairman and chief executive Jack Kahl—who was named one of the 10 "Most Admired CEOs in America" by *Industry Week* magazine in 1993—has set the tone for the company with his "go-the-extra-mile-for-the-customer" philosophy.

The company culture is based on what Kahl calls "service, service, service," and the conviction that servicing the customer well gives Manco the tactical advantage. Kahl maintains that most companies, including many of his competitors, are *not* customer-driven, but rather view the basis of their core competency as development or technology.

From the outside, customer service might seem to be an improbable approach for a company whose bread-and-butter products are "basic consumables" like duct tape and mailer envelopes. But the approach is already paying off. The company has gone from $800,000 in sales in 1971 (when Kahl bought it) to $147 million in 1996. Today, Manco leads the market in several household-product categories, including Duck® tape, which now accounts for 58 percent of all U.S. nontransparent tape sales in the consumer market, and CareMail, an assortment of mailing products. Kahl attributes his success to building "customers for life"—both among retailers who carry and promote Manco products and consumers who wouldn't buy anything else.

"Dale Carnegie in Feathers"

Manco's signature product is Duck® tape. Yes, Duck® tape—spelled the way Kahl heard most consumers pronounce *duct* tape, the generic name for the waterproof, all-purpose sealing tape invented by GIs during World War II from canvas and used for everything from bandaging wounds to patching pup tents.

In the early 1980s, Kahl trademarked the name Duck® tape and designed and adopted a friendly yellow duck as a logo and company mascot. Known as the Manco Duck, it appears on the packaging and display materials of all of the company's products and does double duty as an in-house morale booster. Playing duck for the day at company picnics, parades, parties, and new-store openings is a hotly contested privilege among employees five foot nine and shorter (the size of the costume). So popular is the duck at Christmas parties that Santa has to make his presentation separately, because when the duck shows up, people go crazy. Employees want to touch him and hug him.

Consumers appear to have a similar reaction to the kindly, bug-eyed caricature. Indeed, the Disneyesque duck design was a conscious attempt to establish a memorable link in the minds of Manco customers with its products. "Everything about the duck is non-threatening—warm and friendly," explains Kahl. Indeed the duck was designed for customers—especially women—who want to take the duck under wing. "The duck," exclaims Kahl, "is Dale Carnegie in feathers." It also establishes the right tone for the company and product line, affirming the view of Kahl's mentor Sam Walton—that business should be *fun*.

Headquarters for all this merrymaking is the Manco "campus," just west of Cleveland. Built to resemble loosely Kahl's alma mater, John Carroll University, with a quadrangle and in-building fitness facility (and naturally, its complement of duck ponds), the compound was designed to instill a desire for lifelong learning.

Expanding the mind of the employee to enter the mind of the customer is the end goal in Manco's continuous quest for knowledge. "I have to know more about my customers than I know about myself," Kahl asserts. The process is never ending. Much of it comes from constant communication with its major-company national salespeople, all but two of whom live in Cleveland.

On Thursday—which is "career day"—80 white-collar employees at the privately held company (which is 30 percent employee owned) spend three hours in meetings, divided into morning and after-work sessions. The 7:30 A.M. meeting is devoted to strategic information and "the big picture," or what's going on in the industry globally. At the 5:15 P.M. meeting, tactical information is relayed, with salespeople presenting what they've learned from out in the field. Everyone goes home recharged, in the know, and connected to their work.

Some firms succeed without knowing exactly why, and when the conditions that made them successful in the past change, those firms often collapse. Such firms are not demand-chain leaders. Successful firms that prevail in the *face* of change are those that consciously work to develop and evolve strategies and structures that work well in good times and bad.

This is the case for Manco, the executive committee of which can already see three years into the future. (In today's world of rapid change, Kahl says, it would be hard to see much beyond that.) The foundation of Manco's demand-chain management and customer orientation is its continuous consumer research, including household and individual buying habits and trends. As a result, the company manages to stay not just one step but several steps ahead of where the market is going.

The company uses a range of tools, including focus groups, expert advisory panels, and, most importantly, a consumer hotline, to stay current. The 800 number, instituted in the early 1990s, is "our biggest listening device," says Kahl. With over 8,000 calls ringing in every month (and the number steadily growing), the service costs roughly $150,000 a year—which Kahl considers "dirt cheap" for its immeasurable value. "I see it not as a *cost* but as an investment," he says.

While Manco spends liberally on its help line, it's downright parsimonious with its advertising budget, placing minimal trade and almost zero consumer advertising. Although the company had developed its strategy of brand building without advertising well before the *Harvard Business Review*'s article on the subject, "Building Brands Without Mass Media," appeared in January–February 1997, Kahl was nonetheless delighted to see his ideas confirmed in print.

What information does Manco glean from its 800 callers?

The most common calls are inquiries: Where can I buy this tape? How do you apply weather stripping? Manco operators are trained to dispense expert advice on the entire product line and have a database showing all outlets for the products nationwide. A second sizable group of callers makes suggestions for new uses for existing products or gives new product ideas. This information is systematically entered into the computer database. The last group—the gripers—calls to blow off steam. These comments are also logged into the database for future reference. Company policy dictates that every complainer gets a callback, followed by a letter, and if the customer wants money back, he or she gets it.

The 800 line provides a two-pronged benefit: In addition to giving customers the personal attention they may not have received in the store (while at the same time building brand loyalty), it provides Manco with invaluable, up-to-the-minute feedback. This information is compiled into a five-page monthly report, which summarizes trends, provides anecdotes, and presents graphs. And the department head is encouraged to pop into Kahl's office to relay timely, compelling, or especially poignant items that may come up between the monthly reports.

By listening carefully and attentively to customers, Manco has been able to devise new uses for some of its products. As a result, being tuned into customers' wants has contributed substantially to the company's bottom line.

Listening to a customer led to the creation of a product that's been a bona fide hit—EasyLiner®, a nonadhesive, rollout shelf liner that resembles rubber mesh and is easy to cut, place, and remove. In just three years on the market, the product is already adding $30 million a year to Manco's gross sales figures—and demand continues to soar.

For years, consumers had been lining their kitchen-cabinet shelves and drawers with Contact® paper, a sticky-backed, vinyl paper made by Rubbermaid. Non-mind-to-market firms might have left well enough alone by concluding that since the product was still selling steadily, consumers must be satisfied with it. But Manco paid more attention to consumer comments than to Contact® sales figures and therein seized an opportunity.

The idea for a nonadhering shelf liner came to Manco in January 1994 at a national housewares show in Chicago. A Wal-Mart merchandise manager took Kahl aside and told him: "People hate Contact® paper." The stuff is hard to put down and even harder to take up. Kahl found Jim Hawley, his general manager, and asked the Wal-Mart manager to repeat himself. The Wal-Mart manager had the idea of adapting an existing product—nonskid carpet underliner—as a shelf liner. The two Manco executives knew immediately the enormity of what they were hearing. Kahl and Hawley made an on-the-spot commitment to market the product.

Manco sprang into action with product design, consumer research, and packaging. The company tapped manufacturers already on its demand chain for help and consulted new ones. It took Manco just three months to bring the product from inception to market. EasyLiner® debuted on Wal-Mart's shelves in April of 1994. "Speed under control is what we're all about," says Kahl. "You win races at the Indy 500—and at Manco—that way."

Following on the heels of EasyLiner®, Manco introduced OfficeLiner® and ShopLiner® for use in the office and shop, respectively. OfficeLiner® is identical to EasyLiner® but in "office colors" like gray and almond, while ShopLiner® is a thicker product (used for such things as lining pickup truck beds for the hauling of tools).

The expansion of this product line is far from over. Consumer comments and requests continue to broaden it. One woman called the help line and said EasyLiner® was great beside her swimming pool. That comment and others like it led to a flurry of research (including several fact-finding trips to Germany where a similar product with a variety of applications is already on the market) and a commitment by the company to market an outdoor line. In the spring of 1997, Manco introduced a new outdoor product line, "Moonwalk," including 9-by-12 "rugs" and runners to put down by swimming pools or lay down on wooden decks so that kids don't get splinters while playing.

Manco's development of new products represents a major departure from the role of a wholesaler in the traditional supply chain. By linking the interests of retailers and manufacturers with its own creative talent and unique capabilities in branding, packaging, and logistics and by being proactive in creating solutions to problems, Manco commands its demand chain. These boundary-spanning efforts drive the creation of new, cutting-edge products, which will ensure the company's continued growth and profitability.

Manco also probes the minds of its customers to learn what inventory turns and margins are expected for each item or area of the store, and exactly what it takes in logistics management and information systems to help its retail partners be successful. All members in Manco's demand chain are its *process partners* and contribute to the mission of getting products from the minds of consumers to the marketplace in as little time as possible.

Process Partnership

Process partnership ensures that product design, packaging, displays, promotion, and other elements of the marketing mix meet the requirements of both the retailers and the target consumer market. Probably Manco's earliest major triumph in mind-to-market and speed-to-market success came in 1985, when the company heeded the call for a retail line of mailing products. Just as it would

do nine years later with the EasyLiner® line, Manco made an immediate commitment to bring the product to market. And 90 days
from the day that the company coined the term CareMail, the line
was being shipped to Revco and Wal-Mart.

The company was much smaller at the time, and the staff had to
pull together a demand chain of 60 different vendors (many of
whom they were working with for the first time) to develop the
product line, coordinate the products, and pull everything together
to go to market.

In preparing CareMail, Manco conducted focus groups and
"store intercepts" to find out what consumers wanted in mailing
products. (In a store intercept, researchers observe consumers purchasing a product. As soon as the transactions are complete, they
introduce themselves and conduct an interview about product preferences.) With the CareMail line, for instance, Manco learned to
avoid the colors red, white, and blue (which consumers associated
with the U.S. Postal Service) and stuck with their signature colors of
green and yellow.

The story of the speed to market in the development of
CareMail has already entered company lore and is something of a
benchmark by which management challenges itself to introduce
other products.

By developing new lines like CareMail and EasyLiner, Manco
stakes out its position at the helm of the demand chain. By making
appropriate arrangements with manufacturing partners around the
world, the company serves as a bridge between suppliers and retailers.

Mass retailers as large as Wal-Mart need the technology and
resources of partner companies, most of which cannot supply the
brands, logistics, productivity, and requirements of consumers.
These retailers rely on creative, proactive, visionary firms like
Manco to bring all the partners together in a win-win-win solution.

Because Manco demonstrates many of the qualities needed to lead the demand chain, it has enjoyed rapid growth, even in highly competitive industries (and times). Manco proves that a small firm can use mind-to-market principles to grow and challenge some of the largest and most respected firms in the world, such as Rubbermaid and 3M.

Ultimately, all industrial demand is derived from consumer demand. Any company—be it a manufacturer or intermediary like Manco—that can anticipate and solve problems for its customers becomes far more valuable than firms that merely sell products. Consumer and industrial firms alike would be wise to take a page out of Manco's book and establish ongoing customer support and analysis; in order to succeed in the next millennium, they must be students of consumer behavior and zero in on changing lifestyles and demographics.

BUILDING SUCCESSFUL DEMAND CHAINS

Mind-to-market leadership is a problem-solving approach that your company—no matter what its size or function—can adopt to tap the minds of consumers and deliver products back to the market.

Various strategies exist for building and leading successful demand chains. Some are based on collaboration and strategic partnering; others are based on ownership. For example, The Limited buys many of the necessary components of the chain to maintain control over each entity and thus dominate the chain. Intimate Brands, Inc., a Limited spin-off and parent company of Victoria's Secret Stores, Victoria's Secret Catalog, and Bath & Body Works, owns Gryphon, one of the world's leading producers of personal-care products. In 1996, Gryphon created, packaged, and delivered approximately 300 million units of 2,000 different products, supplying 85 percent of Victoria's Secret and about 75 percent of Bath &

Body Works' bath and fragrance products. Intimate Brands controls its demand chain better by owning a supplier.

When collaboration rather than acquisition is the strategy of choice for building a successful demand chain, management teams from partner firms must agree to make the mutual goal of reaching consumers paramount. Then, they must arrive at a vision of how to do business with each other to serve their customer, while maximizing the strengths that each partner brings to the partnership.

Corporate strategists devote tremendous energy to positioning their firms to assume leadership of existing supply chains and to devising strategies for creating successful demand chains. Firms looking to create such chains must:

- Identify a consumer-driven product or service for the demand chain to create, market, and sell.

- Specify the functions necessary to produce the ultimate output, including production, distribution, retailing, advertising, warehousing, and the like.

- Identify the players and select demand-chain members.

- Develop sources for consumer knowledge and technology, such as connectors, facilitators, and chain members.

- Identify the roles and responsibilities of the players based on their strengths.

- Set goals for the demand chain, so that all members are on the same page in striving to accomplish superior levels of quality, speed, efficiency, cost, and service.

- Find demand-chain partners that share similar values so that a level of trust can be achieved.

THE LITTLE "BANC" THAT COULD

One company that has employed all of the aforementioned principles while evolving from an obscure midwestern bank to become the driving force in a dynamic demand chain is Banc One. The Columbus, Ohio–based bank—which had just $100 million in assets in the early 1960s and now has over $100 billion—transformed the traditional banking supply chain into a demand chain focused on how people prefer to get and spend their money. Along the way, it rewrote the rules of traditional banking and helped to revolutionize an entire industry.

Like Manco, this company has mastered the art of tracking, analyzing, and acting upon customer wants and consumption patterns. It changed its organization to fit the market, and, through the years, has gone to enormous lengths to satisfy customers.

Banc One's success story began in the mid-1960s when it was still called City National Bank and Trust of Columbus (Ohio), or CNB. Though the bank had been around since 1868, it had no capital or legal authority to do business beyond Franklin County lines. But its CEO, John G. McCoy, had a grand vision. Realizing that credit cards could transcend those artificially imposed boundaries, McCoy and a group of colleagues developed a plan and traveled to San Francisco to call on Bank of America, then the world's largest bank. (At the time, Bank of America already distributed a customer credit card in a limited geographic area.) CNB talked the giant into a partnership and the BankAmericard—the forerunner of MasterCard and Visa—was born. CNB developed the concept, collected franchise fees, and offered consumers a kind of financial flexibility they'd never before enjoyed. As a result, CNB became one of the world's leading processors for other banks. This highly profitable venture gave the bank a high price/earnings ratio, propelling it to the forefront of bank holding companies.

In 1968—well before the federal banking laws were changed to permit the formation of bank holding companies and national markets—CNB changed its name to Banc One. (The new name better fit McCoy's vision of his emerging company.) Many executives wait for laws to change before taking action. But visionary leaders, like McCoy, create change in products and organizations and force laws to catch up to them. And, indeed, the changes that he foresaw in his company and in the industry eventually came about.

But these dramatic changes had their seeds in meeting primary customer needs—for such basic things as on-the-spot credit and access to funds.

As if helping to popularize the consumer credit card were not enough, Banc One officials realized that many people wanted to get their money when they shopped, after work and on weekends—not just during the regular banking business hours of 9:00 A.M. to 3:00 P.M., Monday through Friday. At the time, most banks posted their hours and expected customers to work around them. (Some customer-friendlier organizations extended their hours during the week or opened on Saturday mornings.)

So, in 1968, Banc One joined forces with Diebold, a company known for manufacturing bank safes, to develop another product that would advance banking to a new level—the automatic teller machine, or ATM. Banc One's success in this risky venture depended on its ability to read consumer needs, on information about how innovative products "diffuse" (or fan out into the population and gain widespread acceptance), and on support from its supply-chain partners. Banc One unveiled the first ATM in America at the Kingsdale Shopping Center in Columbus in October 1970.

Today, more than a generation later, ATMs are almost as ubiquitous as mailboxes—in part because people expect to have access to their money at all times. The concept has spawned a wave of similar applications. InterBold, a joint venture of Diebold and IBM, currently produces a new wave of multifunction "ATMs" that dispense everything from theater and plane tickets to bus passes and postage stamps.

In addition to bank cards, ATMs, and point-of-sale (or POS) machines in retail stores, Banc One helped to develop and introduce a number of other significant innovations, often against the objections of its banking industry peers. Among them were the first drive-through banking window, computerized overdraft protection, and money-market sweep accounts. What's more, just as Wal-Mart has reframed its self-concept, so too has Banc One, which no longer sees itself as a bank but rather as a "consumer financial center," where people can buy mutual funds, equities, insurance, real estate—just about anything you'd expect to find at a "financial superstore."

Banc One achieved these innovations by forming successful strategic partnerships with some large, well-known firms such as Bank of America, Merrill Lynch, and Diebold, as well as with some smaller firms. (Indeed, innovation is contagious and today abounds all along the demand chain. Diebold, for instance, introduced a new "currency" in the form of stored-value smart cards, which received worldwide attention during the 1996 Summer Olympics when they replaced cash in much of Atlanta.) With the help of its organizational partners, Banc One has grown into a demand-chain leader in the financial-services industry, with its innovations spread far and wide. The company has not only helped to bury the conventional banking industry but has helped to birth exciting new offspring and breathe new life and dynamism into the industry.

A PENNEY IN CHANGE

Mind-to-market leader JCPenney (which in 1996 did more than $19.5 billion in store and catalog sales) continually rethinks its strategies to improve its already intense focus on the consumer. As JCPenney approaches its centennial in 2002, it not only seeks to expand and implement its well-developed mind-to-market strategy but also increasingly to incorporate a corollary principle, speed-to-market.

With over 1,242 stores in all 50 states and Puerto Rico and 3 stores in Latin America, the company is one of the world's largest retailers of apparel, jewelry, accessories, and other products. JCPenney's size—with the largest number of anchor mall positions of any retailer in America—poses an inherent obstacle when it comes to navigating the course of change. To meet the challenge, the company is sharpening all of the competitive instruments at its disposal.

Sometimes a firm is pushed to take radical steps or drastically change direction to keep abreast of the marketplace. Sometimes it pulls ahead of competitors with a market-focused strategy of continual improvement. Both approaches have been used by JCPenney over its many years in the rough-and-tumble wars of apparel and chain department store retailing.

Founded in 1902 by James Cash Penney, the Missouri man whom many consider to be the father of modern chain retailing, JCPenney was from the start an innovator, offering quality merchandise on a cash-only basis and establishing the unprecedented policy of one price for all customers. As the company matured, at times it was forced to change direction and abandon long-standing policies to stay in the game.

Studying the history of major retailers reveals that no matter what its size, every organization must respond to consumer values and realities—bend to the will of the marketplace—or die. During the depression, the JCPenney Company flourished while competitors floundered, in part because of its no-credit policy. Lights went out in stores all over America that accepted checks from banks that folded or extended credit to customers who couldn't pay. By insisting on cash, J. C. Penney kept his company afloat. Penney's cash-oriented organization meshed beautifully with the minds of consumers in the price-obsessed, durability-driven market of the prewar economy. But the company was slow to change its approach when a new consumer mind-set took hold.

During the 1940s and '50s, pent-up consumers (reacting to deprivations of the depression and World War II era) went on a buying binge financed by credit. They purchased not only soft goods "on time" but homes, automobiles, major appliances, and even vacations. Archrival Sears, whose stronghold had long been the catalog business, beat JCPenney to the punch by offering credit to its customers in 1953. Along with its credit cards, Sears invited its legions of catalog customers to visit its giant new store in their neighborhoods.

To the present day, Sears dominates the retail credit-card business. The same policy that was a source of strength for JCPenney in the 1930s proved to be a liability to the company in the 1950s. This is the danger of firms rigidly adhering to fixed positions instead of tailoring their approaches to demographic and psychographic realities. By 1958, Penney relented and offered its own proprietary credit card, but by this time, Sears had already made some serious inroads into its business.

Consumer-Driven Change

In the pre- and postwar environment of large families and limited incomes, JCPenney was the place to shop for clothes to be handed down from one child to the next. The mind of this market focused on durability and conservative styles, and JCPenney provided the perfect environment for this type of retailing. Inarguably, JCPenney benefited from the baby boom that spanned the years 1946 to 1964.

However, in the 1970s and '80s, the consumer landscape changed rapidly and dramatically. W. R. Howell, then CEO, knew that JCPenney had to change, too, or be left behind. Smaller families, urban lifestyles, and higher incomes defined the new environment. For example, with the emergence of the two-paycheck marriage, families were not only more affluent but smaller. With families having only one or two children, the market for "hand-me-downs" virtually disappeared. Families would use clothing until it was tossed out rather than worn out. Durable, conservative items no longer made it in this trendy, disposable era.

A major overhaul, or radical innovation, was in order. JCPenney realized it had to reposition itself—and become a fashion-forward retailer—to keep up with the times.

Kicking the Tires

In 1983, the company embarked on what a company spokesperson has termed an "update and remix" program in which it eliminated its hardware and paint categories and got out of the business of selling automotive parts, major appliances, and lawn and garden items—categories in which Sears held a competitive edge. The tires had to go. Fashionable clothing—including a Halston collection—was added to the practical, conservative lines. And JCPenney embarked on an ambitious remodeling campaign to transform the decor and aesthetic appeal of the stores from functional to inviting.

These changes were steered by extensive consumer research, in which Penney listened to its customers and, in response, began to extend its lines beyond "value-right" merchandise. Although segmentation has always been a component of most retailers' marketing mix (i.e., good, better, best), in preparation for the 1983 overhaul, JCPenney began to study market segments in earnest and offer lines to appeal to different consumers.

Consumer research showed that the JCPenney customer expected good service, and the organization prides itself on delivering it. Sales associates are trained to handle what the company calls its "midlevel" customer by a state-of-the-art distance learning system, which is in place (or soon will be) in all but 90 of the company's 1,242 stores.

Distance learning is what a company spokesperson calls "just down the hall" training. The advantages of JCPenney's in-house distance learning program are legion. If a business problem or need suddenly arises, associates can go to the learning centers in their stores and immediately find "a learning solution." And because the centers have interactive capabilities, managers can participate in training conferences on any number of topics, learning from peers as well as experts. A California store manager might mention a problem broadcast from the Penney Learning Center in Plano, Texas, for example, only to have a solution offered up by an East Coast manager. And that idea might be embellished or refined by the in-studio company expert.

This technology also helps JCPenney continue to "raise the bar" of the company's customer-service level. For instance, the distance learning program recently offered sales associates eight clinics, after which the company saw a noticeable response in sales. The topic of one of the clinics, for instance, was body language. The program showed associates how to mirror the behavior of customers. If the customer is in a hurry, the associate needs to be in a hurry. If the customer is indecisive, or taking her time, so does the associate.

In 1996, JCPenney also began rolling out a companywide CD-ROM system that offers self-paced instruction. New associates must complete an eight-hour "new hire and point-of-sale training program" on the computer before they go out on the floor. The program gives them the JCPenney philosophy of customer service. An in-company Intranet—which provides employees with up-to-the-minute product information—was also rolled out that year.

Investment in all this technology quickly paid for itself. In 1996, JCPenney stopped flying employees to Texas for training and halted publishing, warehousing, and mailing training programs. It put those dollar savings into technology and recouped its investment in equipment within a year.

From Arizona to St. John's Bay

Just as JCPenney is investing heavily in employee training, it's making the same smart choices in product development.

The company is trying to understand both from the big picture and on a micromarketing and micromerchandising level the many life stages and lifestyles that its customers express in the way they furnish their homes and cover their bodies. To that end, JCPenney uses the Internet, in-store research, and focus groups to understand what customers want and why. It seeks to tailor its private branding program along with its selection of national brands to meet customer needs.

As customers spin off into smaller and smaller market segments, savvy marketers are being challenged to meet their needs and wants with new brands. Behaving as a sort of department store of "boutiques"—each one appealing to a different market segment—JCPenney's challenge is to attract an increasingly varied set of customers to its "umbrella."

For example, two consumer hot spots of the moment for JCPenney are Arizona and St. John's Bay—not the vacation destinations but the brand names, which represent fun-filled lifestyles and business-casual office styles respectively.

Six hundred to eight hundred consumers or potential customers of the line are shown each category of merchandise while it's still in its development stages. They're asked to evaluate styling, price, and fabrication. The heaviest consumer research is done for the company's stronghold: its private-label lines. Numerous changes are made to the products between the time they're tested and the time they land on the floor.

Consumer research tells JCPenney that workers—especially men—are baffled by how to dress appropriately on dress-down Fridays and for "business-casual" occasions. In years past, it was easy: Businessmen had five suits and a couple of ties that they knew went together and rotated them. But in today's business-casual setting, many customers need help in putting the right look together so that they won't look like they just wandered in off the golf course.

JCPenney's line, Options by Stafford, is targeted at precisely this consumer. It's the adult male version of the 1970s clothing brand Garanimals—a children's line in which tops and bottoms could be matched by lining up two tags sporting lions, giraffes, or elephants. All the components in the Options by Stafford line match everything in it. The company views it as a successful launch.

Listening to consumers has helped the company develop new lines. But in order to achieve marketing success with so large and varied an organization, the company will ultimately have to tailor its merchandise mix to each individual market. Therefore, JCPenney's long-term objective is to achieve "mass customization." That is an approach in which each store gets just the right merchandise, just the right colors and sizes, just in time. The mix sent to each store will be customized to correspond with that store's strengths and weaknesses in various niches or lines, as well as to its demographics and psychographics. Three to five years is the company's "best guess" on achieving this objective. If this rollout goes according to plan, JCPenney will serve as a mind-to-market model for mass merchandisers.

What's Happening in Plano?

Engraved on a clock in the conference room of JCPenney's Plano, Texas, headquarters, the words *JCPenney 2002: The Speed of Change* serve as a constant reminder of the challenges and goals JCPenney faces as it enters the new millennium. In January 1997, James E. Oesterreicher succeeded W. R. Howell as chairman of the board. As chairman, he will carry out many of the goals he and his management team set when he became CEO three years earlier, including a commitment to be responsive to market trends and to give consumers what they want.

In today's overstored retail environment, a mind-to-market focus must emphasize not only consumer inclusion but speed to market in distribution and logistics. If black jumpers are hot, JCPenney must have them on the racks in no time. To that end, Oesterreicher has made one of the major goals of the company to reduce product development and distribution cycle times.

But no matter how well the in-store retailing environment is managed, JCPenney, Sears, and their competitors will have to focus on keeping their supply chains efficient, swift, and cost-effective in order to thrive in the hypercompetitive markets of the future. Perhaps a logistics and distribution system overhaul will be the radical innovation that propels JCPenney back into consistent strong earnings in the next decade. While starting with the consumer is important in building demand chains, without intense focus on getting products to the market cost-effectively and with lightning speed, long-term profitability of all demand-chain organizations is jeopardized.

FAIL TO PLAN, PLAN TO FAIL

Failing organizations pay little attention to the changes occurring around them. Instead, they focus on tactics to reach existing markets or market segments, dwelling on past successes rather than future plans. These backward-looking organizations often give little more than lip service to the need to anticipate markets of the future. They fail to monitor continuously the environment and select dynamic market segments, and they lack adaptive marketing strategies.

In contrast, mind-to-market leaders focus keenly on the future. When people in all areas of the organization share knowledge about consumption patterns of the present and the future, as well as share a common vision of tomorrow's markets, they're better equipped to change. With a single statement, Lou Gerstener committed IBM to a mind-to-market future when, on the day the new CEO took office, he pronounced: "We must stop looking inward. From now on we will look outward."

Mind-to-market leaders possess the ability to change not only themselves but the entire supply chain to meet the needs of the ever-emerging market. Indeed, mind-to-market leaders program their entire organizational structure for ongoing, continuous improvement. Such gradual and subtle changes in strategies, which are tied to marketplace realities, are far more efficient than sudden shifts, massive overhauls, and attempts to play "catch-up."

What's more, continuous improvement campaigns often go

unnoticed (and undetected by competitors) whereas chaotic changes send a red-flag signal to competitors. Eastern Airlines, for instance, in its final years as a commercial carrier, was notorious for trying a number of desperation strategies, including cutting fares below cost. Needless to say, nothing worked.

LEARNING FROM THE PAST AND LOOKING TO THE FUTURE

From the 1960s until recently, large retailers dominated the channels of distribution, or supply chains. First it was Sears and A & P. Later, Kmart, Wal-Mart, Toys "R" Us, The Limited, and others. As strong as many of these players are now, in the ever-changing picture of the business world, the past is never more than a prologue for the future. The entire landscape will be different in the new millennium.

Some successful firms do things right. Some successful firms do the right things. Mind-to-market leaders do the right things right. Whether it's the speed and efficiency at Manco, the demand-chain partnerships at Banc One, or the consumer-driven changes at JCPenney, getting the details right in the demand chain is required for success in the marketplace. Mind-to-market leadership requires knowledge of customer minds and certain types of organizational structures—topics described in the rest of this book.

Søren Kierkegaard, the great Danish philosopher, observed that life must be lived forward, but can only be understood backwards. When applied to the business environment, only the future will tell us who'll be in charge of the demand chain of tomorrow.

two

MEETING THE NEEDS OF TODAY'S CONSUMERS

"The mind, once expanded to the dimensions of larger ideas, never returns to its original size."

— Oliver Wendell Holmes

BEYOND BUYER BEHAVIOR

In order to thrive in the hypercompetitive climate of the future, manufacturers, wholesalers, retailers, and every entity along the demand chain must step outside of their comfort zones and take care of the first order of any business transaction—namely, understanding consumer needs. Quite simply, businesses will have no choice but to analyze and understand the minds of the end users of every product that's made and every service that's offered, thus becoming the foundation for the entire demand chain.

To achieve mind-to-market mastery, business leaders and CEOs must push their understanding of the customer beyond mere buyer behavior (knowing *what* people buy) into the realm of consumption behavior (knowing *why* people buy), how they buy and how emotional components and lifestyle factors contribute to the transaction. Understanding *consumption behavior* will provide insight into the inner recesses of consumer minds; once there, you can better determine how to meet customers' needs and wants best. This is the starting point of building a demand chain.

While understanding buyer behavior may aid your company in selling existing products within current channels of distribution, those who understand consumption behavior can actually create value with new or improved products and restructured distribution channels. But first you need to know where to start.

A ROAD MAP OF THE MIND

You've just arrived at the airport in a strange city and have rented a car to get to your hotel. If you don't know how to get there, you're left with two choices: use a set of directions detailing the roads you need to take (left on Birchtree Circle through two traffic lights, right on Thomasville Road for 3.4 miles, etc.), or study a road map and figure it out on your own. At first glance, using a set of directions would seem easier. And, most of the time, it is. But what happens when you hit a detour, need to make an emergency stop, or simply get lost along the way? In that case, a series of out-of-context street names won't get you there. It helps to have a sense of where you're headed so you can make it on your own. By charting your own course, you'll both understand the big picture and get to where you want to be.

In the disruptive, discontinuous markets of contemporary and future business environments, a "road map" of how consumers make purchase decisions is much more reliable than working from someone else's set of directions.

Understanding consumer decisions is a process used by many mind-to-market leaders, such as Ford, Kinko's, and Nike, to find a path to the future. A road map (albeit condensed) of how consumers make decisions is shown in Figure 2.1.

MEETING A "NEED"

The starting point for any purchase decision is a customer problem, need, or wish. Consumers don't just walk into stores and say, "You have things to sell. I have some money I'd like to spend. Pick some-

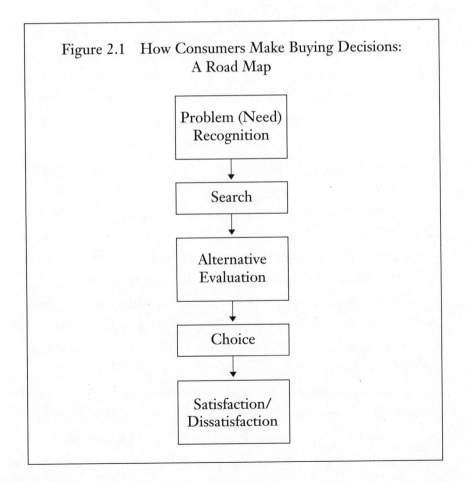

Figure 2.1   How Consumers Make Buying Decisions:
A Road Map

Problem (Need) Recognition

Search

Alternative Evaluation

Choice

Satisfaction/ Dissatisfaction

thing out for me and charge it to my credit card." Consumers buy things for specific reasons—when they believe a product's ability to meet a need is worth more than the cost of buying it. Therefore, the first step toward a sale is identifying a problem or recognizing an unmet need. While this may seem elementary, far too often businesses start the product development process based on what they are able to make or sell rather than basing the process on satisfying customers' wants and needs. Regardless of the degree of wow-factor, a product launch will never be successful unless the new product meets a preexisting and prevalent consumer need better than the existing products on the market.

Eastman Kodak Co.'s decision to introduce "special-use cameras" is a prime example of a company responding appropriately to a demonstrable consumer need. Kodak created this new product after years of hearing consumer complaints and suggestions from people who'd traveled away from home only to find that they'd forgotten their cameras. They wanted pictures to show off back home, but didn't want to purchase another "real" camera. In 1987, the company introduced its one-time-use cameras, which include the regular land model as well as underwater and panorama versions. Kodak focused on how consumers wanted to use the cameras and solved the problems that the hazards of sea, sun, and sand presented. Kodak watched sales of these cameras skyrocket from 5 million in 1987 to 50 million by 1996. (Kodak shuns the word "disposable" to describe the product because, in fact, it sends the camera shell after its use to a central processing facility where components are removed and recycled.)

What prevents many new products from finding a secure home in the market is the absence of such a genuine customer need. No matter how dazzling or original the technology or how many promotional dollars are spent trying to convince consumers to buy something, products and services that don't solve consumer problems invariably fall short. Just look at Viewtron, a TV set–top box that when paired with a converter allowed consumers to scan the news each morning via their TV sets and self-select programming to match their interests.

Introduced into the U.S. market in 1980, the idea had been developed in Europe over an 11-year period, and, when brought to the United States, was a joint venture between AT&T and the newspaper chain Knight-Ridder. Though the product employed state-of-the-art technology and was visionary in its attempt to create an on-call, interactive kind of "newspaper," Viewtron forced customers to do more work than they wanted to. In addition, they had to pay a whopping $800 for the converter box, program the machine, stay in one place to watch its offerings, and fork over a hefty monthly subscriber fee.

While Viewtron sounded great to the techies and executives who appropriated millions to create, distribute, and sell this precursor to the Internet, neither the product nor the distribution channel filled a void for general consumers in the home. People could scan headlines of the low-tech (paper) newspaper more quickly than they could activate the Viewtron, and the former provided news junkies with detail not found in the encapsulated TV version. What's more, traditional newspapers were cheap and portable—they could be "scanned" in the bathroom, at the breakfast table, or even on the bus to work. Technologically, the Viewtron product was superior, but it failed because consumers were not experiencing the problem it intended to solve.

A version of the Viewtron story repeated itself a decade later when the sophisticated powerhouse companies IBM and Sears reportedly invested over $2.5 billion in a joint venture for a company called Prodigy. The premise was simple—mass-market consumers could shop on their computers plus get a sampling of other information such as stock quotes, sports, and news. But once again, the product failed because mass-market consumers were not unhappy with their current method of shopping and because those who owned computers and modems represented only a small fraction of the total population (and their information needs were highly specialized).

PRODUCT FAILURE

Failing to perform the function it was designed to accomplish is rarely the reason for a new product's failure. Generally, products fail because the problems engineers design products to solve are not always perceived as real problems by consumers. Many of the thousands of new products that clutter retail shelves every year fail because they were designed to solve a manufacturer's need for sales growth rather than a consumer problem. In fact, the reason for these failures is a lack of attention to the demand chain. Not only has the proliferation of unneeded products hurt manufacturers, but it has devastated retailers who added too many stock keeping units (or SKUs) and expanded stores beyond the size of profitability.

Other reasons for product failure:

- The product may solve an important problem but is not substantially different so as to induce consumers to switch from an existing product or supplier to a new one.

- The product is sold through an inconvenient or inefficient supply chain that makes acquisition difficult.

- The product may have an adequate distribution channel but fail because the marketer is ineffective in communicating why its product is superior to the alternatives.

THE BUYING PROCESS

When consumers have identified a need or a want and have decided to devote money, time, energy, and attention to purchasing an item or service, an automatic yet complicated process ensues. To stay in business in the hypercompetitive climate of today and tomorrow, you must understand every phase of a consumer's decision-making process.

The "Search"

Once a consumer recognizes a need or a problem, the search process begins, with the consumer identifying possible strategies and products to satisfy the unmet need. Sometimes, consumers search passively, their receptivity to information around them merely becoming heightened. Or the "search" may begin slowly, with the person rummaging through ideas from his or her memory bank. Still other times, the search process is active right from the start, with a consumer paying attention to ads, researching consumer publications such as *Consumer Reports*, and launching out on shopping trips, etc.

Consumer variables such as personality, social class, income, and purchase size certainly affect the length and depth of the search. Past experiences with products also come into play. If a consumer is happy with the product he or she currently uses, he may not search at all for a replacement, but simply go back to the outlet where the last one was purchased to buy the latest model. But if consumers are unhappy with a current product or brand, the search expands.

Some consumers enjoy looking. Walking and browsing through malls and stores is fun for them, while for others, it's a headache-producing chore. Understanding when the search is fun and when it's tiresome—and for whom—provides businesspeople with invaluable information when constructing demand chains.

For example, the search for a microwave oven doesn't excite many consumers. The most effective marketing channel in this instance minimizes the time and effort required to get product information. That's why Best Buy, one of America's largest appliance and electronics retailers, scatters video kiosks throughout the store—to provide quick, in-depth information. By contrast, the search for an evening dress is likely to be an altogether different experience. Browsing, trying on different styles, and modeling the garment before the dressing-room mirror may bring pleasures of fantasy, association, and anticipation. In this case, the experience is not only visual but personal, and the customer may want to prolong rather than shorten the buying process.

One reason that catalogers have cut into retailers' sales is that they simplify the search process for customers by providing more information than typically found in a store. Victoria's Secret, for instance, dominates the catalog field for lingerie and sexy nightwear. Part of its appeal is that its catalogs are both exciting and informative. Consumers can examine fabric, style, and color alternatives quickly, at any time of the day or night and in any room of their home. And with the immediacy of an 800 number, they can determine whether a product is in stock in the desired color and size and find out how long it will take to arrive.

Consumers' search behaviors impact businesses of all sizes. At Marriott, measurement programs—ranging from in-room comment cards to frequent-traveler surveys—identify which customers are searching for alternatives to which problems. The company's research also encompasses noncustomers so that it can identify unmet needs and, in the process, extend its potential consumer base. By adopting information-gathering strategies like Marriott's, mind-to-market leaders can ambush a competitor, hijack its customers, and displace its products, methods of selling, or even its supply chain.

When a company reaches noncustomers and gives them product information and alternatives, they have hit pay dirt. Noncustomers, after all, have the potential of becoming customers for life.

Evaluating Alternatives

"What are my options? Which is best?" Consumers constantly seek answers to such questions in the "alternative-evaluation" stage, when they compare, contrast, and select from various products or services. Although this process is intertwined with both the search and choice processes, understanding it as a prepurchase evaluation aids in designing marketing strategies. During alternative evaluation, consumers compare what they know about different products and brands with what they consider most important. In the end, they resolve to buy one of them.

Precisely how do consumers evaluate alternatives?

Consumers choose products, services, and stores based on the attributes most important to them. Among the most important attributes—what marketing experts call the *"salient" characteristics*—are price, basic characteristics, reliability, and quality. For instance, in the case of a vehicle, the salient attributes would determine which category you were buying—whether an economy sedan, a luxury automobile, a sports utility vehicle, or a pickup truck. But surprisingly, it's what experts call the *"determinant" attributes*—details like color, instrument display-panel configuration, the nap of the upholstery fabric, and even cupholder size—that often as not determine the purchase. When most manufacturers and retailers achieve equivalence on most salient characteristics such as price, reliability, and quality, the difference is in the details.

Details such as these will determine who'll win the store wars of the new millennium. For retailers, the "details" are such things as friendliness, convenience, clean rest rooms, having the right products on the shelf at the right time, speed at the checkout counter, and a host of other things that exist in consumers' experience (and linger in their minds) that determine what and where they buy. For the manufacturer, product details, such as how many cupholders a sport utility vehicle has, will help push a customer to the brink of purchase.

Making the Purchase

A consumer might move seamlessly through the first three stages—perceiving a problem, searching for information, and evaluating alternatives—but stop short at the purchase stage of taking the final step. This last stage is the critical juncture, the time when the chips are down and the deal is sealed or broken. (Not infrequently, after the consumer has decided in his or her mind to buy a particular product or brand—because of what happens during this final stage—he or she ends up buying something quite different or decides not to buy at all.)

Consumers move through the purchase stage in two phases. In phase one, they select one retailer over another (or some other form of retailing such as catalogs, direct sales, or TV- or PC-assisted electronic sales). The second phase involves making in-store choices, which are influenced by salespersons, product displays, electronic media, and point-of-purchase (or POP) advertising.

A consumer may prefer one retailer but choose another because of a sale or a promotional event at a competitor, or due to hours of operation, location, or traffic-flow problems of the moment. Inside the store, the consumer may talk with a salesperson who changes his or her mind, may see an end-of-aisle display that switches the brand preference, use a coupon or price discount, fail to find the intended product or brand, or lack the money or proper credit card to complete the transaction. Mind-to-market leaders must micromanage all aspects of the in-store shopping experience so that the overall attributes and image of the retail environment will achieve preferred patronage and desired sales outcomes.

And they must follow the lead of star performers, such as the Seattle-based Nordstrom, which are known for customer-oriented sales and service. (Nordstrom's highly touted sales force has a stellar record at converting consumer intentions into purchases.)

In the past, retailers succeeded without making much effort to influence consumers at any stage except purchase. Retailers generally left it to manufacturers to develop new products, determine product attributes, advertise brands, and take the lead in marketing activities outside the store. But in tomorrow's demand-chain environment, retailers and manufacturers will need to work together to help each other succeed. Retailers now focus on the early stages of consumer decision making as well as the purchase phase, while manufacturers are taking on more responsibility for what happens inside the store. Manufacturers offer programs to train salespeople, install store fixtures, and offer POP materials. In the new millennium, persuading consumers to buy the products of one manufacturer or one retailer will increasingly require the team efforts of manufacturer, retailer, and other entities on the demand chain, all of which are focused on every stage of consumer decision making.

But Do I Really Like It?

The final stage of consumer decision making is the postpurchase phase. Satisfaction or dissatisfaction. Postpurchase euphoria or postpurchase blues. Consumers store their evaluations in memory banks and retrieve them for future decisions regarding the same or similar items. If the consumer is highly satisfied with her purchase and exhibits no postpurchase blues, the next go-round is likely to become much shorter. Satisfaction increases a consumer's propensity to buy the same brand at the same store.

The higher the price, the more frequently people second-guess their purchase decisions. In psychological terminology, it's called cognitive dissonance. Firms are increasingly developing strategies to allay postpurchase jitters. Manco and many others now have 800 numbers to answer consumer questions, and it's also become increasingly common for companies to provide hang-tags and informational brochures to accompany their products. Some car companies are now routinely following up with a phone call a day or so after the sale to confirm that customers are satisfied with their purchase and to provide them with reassurance. Mind-to-market leadership starts by understanding the problems or unmet needs of consumers but achieves success by delivering solutions that delight consumers to achieve long-term loyalty to the brand or store.

KNOWING WHERE TO "SCRATCH": CONSUMER BUDGETS

In order to avoid such failures and succeed with a new product, marketers must understand consumers' needs. If you know where people itch, you have a better idea of where to scratch with new and improved products and services, more effective communications, and more user-friendly distribution channels.

In the past, the focus for attracting new customers has always centered on their financial resources: How much do customers have to spend and how much are they willing to pay for an item? But in today's age of time famine and two-paycheck marriages, most consumers actually have several significant "budgets" to consider. And perceptive businesspeople must broaden their marketing approach to take into consideration consumers' allocations of precious resources other than money.

Paramount among them are people's *time budgets*, which have become increasingly strapped in our age of overwork. Indeed, many Americans value time so much that they'd gladly trade money for time (if only they could). As a result, most people are willing to throw only so much time at a problem for which a product may provide a solution. Additionally, marketers need to factor consumers' energy and attention budgets into the overall marketing equation.

Just as marketers compete for consumers' limited money and time, they also compete for their attention. Walk through a supermarket, and you'll see consumers scanning shelves, comparing labels, and often looking a bit dazed. What they're doing is spending their precious cognitive capacity processing information. Since we can only process so much information at any given time, marketers would be wise to simplify their messages both in an effort to break through the sensory clutter as well as to help consumers make intelligent product choices quickly and easily.

Visionary marketers classify consumer resources into three "budget" types: economic, temporal, and cognitive. The greenbacks consumers spend on a specific product or in a certain store depend upon their income levels and savings rates as well as the overall economic climate. Because lifestyles directly affect how consumers spend their resources, successful entrepreneurs and managers build demand chains based on understanding the interplay between the two.

THE "TIFFANY/WAL-MART" STRATEGY

The age of Aquarius has been displaced by the age of income inequality. The "haves" are becoming more affluent and the "have-nots" less so. During the past decade, the top 5 percent of the population experienced an increase in real income of over 35 percent, while the income of the wealthiest fifth of our nation grew during that same period by almost 25 percent. While the next quintile gained nearly 10 percent in real income, the income of the bottom 60 percent remained flat or declined slightly. Perhaps the most significant of all developments is that the real income of the middle class is flat or declining at a time when its numbers are shrinking. All of these trends are expected to expand in the future.

How can businesses respond?

Savvy marketers are pursuing the so-called "Tiffany/Wal-Mart" strategy to selling goods and services in our emerging two-tiered economy. Both down-market companies like Consolidated Stores and upscale department stores like Bloomingdale's and Nordstrom are expected to profit from successfully targeting these respective markets. Opportunities will abound for everyone who understands niche marketing and how to reach the customer at his or her socio-economic home base.

TARGETING THE "UP" MARKET

High quality and good service dominate the consumption decisions of up-market customers. And while affluent consumers represent only 20 percent of the market, they now control 55 percent of total personal income, a proportion that has been steadily increasing in recent years. In fact, that number jumped from 50 percent in 1990.

Affluent consumers are often both intelligent and enterprising when it comes to making purchasing decisions. They may not buy the lowest price, but they seek the highest value. Look inside their wallets and you'll likely find a Sears credit card alongside a Saks Fifth Avenue and American Express gold card. Stocked with an ample inventory of goods and services, affluent consumers can wait until the retailer, or the mind-to-market chain, produces and sells exactly what they want. They know how to ask for and track down products—even if it means getting on the phone and researching them and having them mailed from distant points. Given the rapid expansion of the affluent segment, a trend that will undoubtedly continue to increase, marketers to these "top-tier" consumers will have to develop improved products, more informative communication methods, better trained service personnel, and more convenient and user-oriented operating policies.

Crossovers

But income doesn't always determine behavior. Up-market customers seem to relish crossing over to shop at discounters and resale shops; by the same token, down-market consumers are occasionally capable of buying designer labels—often for special occasions and sometimes at full price. While such crossover shopping occurs less frequently than traditional buying patterns, smart marketers must understand that crossover potential is real, and it's occurring more than ever before. Treating all consumers with respect and offering value—that is, good products at reasonable prices—is the way to target this potentially influential market as one.

TARGETING THE VALUE MARKET

It's not just a question of purchasing power—it's customer service across the board. Even down-market consumers expect (and often demand) to have their needs met in the marketplace. They want high value from the retailers they patronize, and expect stores to be pleasant and user-friendly. Successful marketers treat this segment with kid gloves. "Nobody wants to be reminded that they are not rich," market researcher Sanford Goodkin once observed. "Successful discounters have made their mark by convincing customers they are smart and special, not poor riffraff."

The Odd Lots/Big Lots chain—the purveyor of closeout items—is a prime example of a retailing entity that targets the lower tier of our two-tier marketplace. By going the extra mile to meet consumer expectations, it has been able to grow its business and become the country's largest closeout retailer with 614 stores.

Enter an Odd Lots store (it's called Big Lots in some regions) and your treasure hunt begins. Consumers morph into modern-day pirates, exploring aisles packed with closeout treasures. They roll up their sleeves and hunt for this week's specials, making each shopping experience unique and in some cases exciting. Part of the excitement is that customers never know what they'll find. One day it might be paper towels and cereal. On another, they might luck upon an assemble-it-yourself entertainment center or an IBM computer. For these treasures, they're likely to pay half of the retail price— and, in many cases, far less.

In 1990, when CEO William Kelley took over the helm of the Columbus, Ohio–based Consolidated Stores, of which Odd Lots is its largest division, he resolved to upgrade the chain to make it more consumer-friendly. As a result, the chain broadened its consumer base, and has seen annual sales shoot up every year since. (In 1990, net earnings for the then seven-year-old chain rose by a whopping *342 percent.*) In 1996, sales hit $2.7 billion and, in the first quarter of 1997, comparable store sales increased by 18 percent—significantly outpacing Wal-Mart, Target, and Sears. In addition to Odd Lots, Consolidated owns Kay-Bee Toys (the second-largest toy retailer in America after Toys "R" Us, which it acquired in 1996), Toy Liquidators, and Toys Unlimited. (The company has closed its ¡TZADEAL! and All For One divisions.)

Consolidated buys and "consolidates" excess inventory from manufacturers and other retailers at distressed prices. Its network of 1,798 stores in 50 states can absorb huge amounts of inventory, giving it extraordinary bargaining power in the channel. Because it often buys items at pennies on the dollar and because its logistics systems, including distribution and warehousing, are lean and efficient, the company is able to pass dramatic savings along to value-conscious customers.

But just because merchandise is marked at bargain-basement prices, Kelley reasoned, doesn't mean that its display should be sloppy, schlocky, or disrespectful. As a result, Kelley made a primary goal of transforming Odd Lots stores from dingy and depressing to light, bright, clean, and attractive. A big part of the job was eliminating randomly strewn merchandise and creating a logical internal flow. Today, wares are carefully organized into such sections as soft goods, hard goods, and hardware. Even though the merchandise mix varies daily, customers now know where to go to search out their heart's desire. As a result, the store has been able to attract bargain hunters of all economic stripes, including middle-class and affluent shoppers—recreational shoppers who shop for the thrill of stumbling onto a deal.

Young adults, or Generation Xers, also make up a core group of the down-market consumers who turn to Odd Lots to meet their expanding needs within straitened budgets. Financially strapped young consumers don't seem to mind that the merchandise is not consistent. Since they're often just setting up housekeeping and need virtually everything, they prove to be ideal customers. Indeed, low prices attract customers into Odd Lots stores, but value, service, curiosity—and sport—bring them back.

"Off-Price" Consumers

Odd Lots customers are part of a new generation of consumers who emerged during the last decade, a generation of "off-price" buyers who don't expect to pay full price for anything ever again. Constant sales and discounting have created these price-obsessed consumers. This attitude is most entrenched among Generation Xers but has been adopted by other age groups, including those who grew up paying full price at department stores and elsewhere. "Tiffany shoppers" are also, in many cases, patronizing these untraditional outlets due to the "upscaling" of the stores, the "high" they experience from "getting a deal," and the pervasive influence of the Kmarts, Wal-Marts, and Targets throughout our culture.

Ultimately, retailers have only themselves to blame for this attitude. Once the discounting of new merchandise and the holding of weekly "sales" becomes standard practice, it can be difficult to put an end to it. If left unchecked, this off-price mentality will yield lower total retail revenues. Retailers who have what consumers want must behave like parents practicing a form of "tough love" and refuse to succumb to constant price-cutting pressures. Although this is easier said than done (according to those retailers who have watched as some consumers have simply gone to other retailers in search of sale prices), only this kind of strictness can create desired change in the long run. The key is having, in the store, the products for which consumers are willing to pay full price. For mind-to-market leaders like Nike and JCPenney that means creating strong brands that not only command consumers' attention but also their dollars.

THE VALUE OF TIME

To survive in the new millennium, firms must study consumers' time styles to learn how they allocate time among various activities and where shopping fits into the picture. While financial budgets come in a variety of sizes, we all know that time budgets come in "one size fits all." Consumers who have the most money frequent stores that are open when they want to shop. High-income, time-starved consumers especially resent stores, banks, and other firms that charge high "time" prices, including time spent parking and waiting on line. Retailers like Meijer and ServiceMaster who figure out strategies to reduce their "time charges" will dominate the marketplace in the 21st century.

BROTHER CAN YOU SPARE SOME TIME?

Many of today's consumers would readily substitute some time for the desired "dime" immortalized in this famous depression-era song. In the past, consumer time budgets were divided into two basic categories—work and leisure. A more realistic, contemporary view of time consists of three components—paid time, obligated time, and discretionary time.

Paid time represents time at work, which occupies an increasing portion of most people's time budgets. To make ends meet, many Americans are working longer hours or taking on extra jobs. *Obligated time* (or nondiscretionary time) is time earmarked for sleep and economic, legal, moral, or social obligations. It's time you commit to do things that you often wish you didn't have to do. *Discretionary time* is devoted to leisure and family—a shrinking portion of most people's time budgets. Figure 2.2 examines how consumers allocate their time budgets and helps businesses predict which goods and services are most likely to grow in the coming century of the consumer.

High-income earners experience time famine for two reasons: They tend to work more hours than others and they commit to more obligations. Among very high income consumers such as entrepreneurs, managers, and professionals, 60- to 70-plus-hour workweeks are the norm. But just because they have less leisure time

Figure 2.2   The New Way to Analyze Time Budgets

Traditional Concepts of Time and Leisure (24 hours)

WORK	LEISURE

Contemporary Concepts of Time and Leisure (24 hours)

WORK	NONDISCRETIONARY TIME	LEISURE
"Paid Time"	"Obligated Time"	"Discretionary Time"

doesn't mean they don't exploit every leisure moment that comes their way. In fact, this demographic segment buys as many thrills per hour as possible and is willing to pay handsomely to enjoy these "stolen moments" in the form of guided hikes up Mount Everest, vacations on private islands, and African safaris. They're also willing to pay for the best accoutrements for their adventures, including space-age ski, golf, and tennis equipment. Personal fitness trainers and coaches are often squeezed into an already packed schedule in an effort to hone their skills and sculpt their bodies.

Harried Americans cope with their time-crunched lifestyles in numerous ways. About 38 percent cut back on sleep as a way to "make" more time. Many consumers—especially women—spend less time doing housework, cooking, and general home maintenance than in the past. As a general rule, it appears that people decrease the amount of time they spend doing things they find unpleasant.

Multitasking is another common time-saving strategy. If you watch TV, talk on the phone, and pay bills simultaneously, or drive, eat, and listen to an audiotape at the same time, you, too, are a multitasker. Multitasking, or polychronic time usage, involves doing different things at the same time. The TV generation grew up with a diet of this behavior and they're inclined to embrace a product that makes it possible to watch TV on a corner of their computer screen while they work.

When it comes to shopping, consumers with overextended time budgets are likely to favor smaller shops, strip malls, or one-stop shopping concepts over large, congested shopping malls; they're likely to spend less time comparing prices than other consumers; they may also use technology to reduce transaction time and will often consider alternative forms of buying to save time and energy. These "alternatives" include catalog and electronic shopping on the Internet, as well as direct sales approaches. Harried consumers also consider fewer brands, and once they've found a brand that satisfies them, they're likely to stick with it.

BRAND STRATEGY

Because of the dual realities of proliferating product choices and consumers' shrinking time, energy, and attention budgets, brand names will become an even more useful tool for marketers in the future. Good brands are symbols, or endorsements that effectively communicate to consumers the special attributes of products. Sales displays scream "buy me," but brand names serve as shorthand for the rationale in making the purchase. Brands such as Gillette, McDonald's, and Levi's convey a set of expectations, make a promise about a product, and offer a context for trust. When consumers are satisfied with a brand, they come to rely on it and thus feel little need to look elsewhere. In effect, brand loyalty helps reduce people's shopping time.

Great brands, ranging from the venerable Coca-Cola to more recent ones such as Wendy's and Starbucks, are the most valuable assets these firms own. They have far more value than the bricks and mortar listed on these companies' balance sheets. If a company snags a loyal consumer segment, it should do whatever possible to maintain a consistent level of quality, rather than lose this segment and spend precious time and resources trying to win new customers. This is an important focus of mind-to-market leaders' thinking about competing in the future.

Private Labels

Private labels increasingly perform the same function for consumers as manufacturers' brands. In the United States, retailers have traditionally positioned their private labels as the low-price alternative to national manufacturer brands. Rather than competing in the quality arena, American private labels have competed mostly on price, but that too is changing.

The Canadian grocer Loblaws came up with an alternative strategy. It developed a store brand called President's Choice that offers highly attractive upscale packaging and quality products that equal or surpass most national brands. As a result, President's Choice became one of the most trusted and recognized brands in Canada. Leading American retailers now import the brand because of its quality products ranging from cookies to cola. As demand chains learn to position private-label products based on superior quality and attractive packaging, the line between national manufacturer brands and retailers' private labels will begin to blur, offering retailers the loyalty consumers used to reserve for national brands (which could be purchased at competing retail outlets) and the higher margins that come with store brands.

The Meijer League

A thriving, pioneering company that was light-years ahead of its time, so to speak, in catering to time-sensitive customers is the Meijer (pronounced to rhyme with "buyer") chain, a midwestern supermarket-cum-discounter. The company started in 1934 as a single grocery store in Greenville, Michigan. But the winning formula was born in October 1961, when Hendrik Meijer announced the marriage of a supermarket and a discount department store under one roof spanning two acres. A revolution in retailing, Thrifty Acres was born in the spring of 1962—the same year that Kmart opened its doors. Thrifty Acres took the discount retailing concept a step further than its competitors, successfully selling groceries, hardware, clothing, housewares, and more under that one roof. It took decades for such giants as Wal-Mart and Kmart to adopt a similar strategy, which they have yet to master.

When Meijer customers change, it changes with them. Open 24 hours a day, Meijer focuses on customer lifestyles and timestyles to offer fresh, exotic produce, tasty meals to go, and quality clothing as well as popular toys and appliances—all under a single, one-stop-shopping umbrella. Now headquartered in Grand Rapids, it has grown into a 107-store chain of 100,000-plus-square-foot stores dotted throughout the suburbs and small towns of the Midwest. Though protected behind the veil of private ownership, Meijer's growth and profits are said to be exceptional.

Meijer based its time-sensitive strategy on its understanding of customer demographics and lifestyles. In many of the Michigan cities where Meijer prospered early on, high-income factory employees worked shifts that ended in the wee hours of the night. Many customers with money in those cities did not and could not shop during regular daytime hours; when they did shop, they wanted to buy more than just groceries. While competitors slept, Meijer learned a lesson well—do business according to your customers' schedules, not your own. In 1969, it opened its stores on Sundays; the following year, it extended its hours from 7:00 A.M. to 11:00 P.M.; and, in 1988, it opened its stores 24 hours a day.

Yesterday's factory workers are today's high-income professionals and entrepreneurs who work long hours and cannot shop when most stores are open. Two-income households are the norm today, often with partners working different shifts. And three-income families (when two partners share three jobs between them) are not uncommon.

Throughout the years, Meijer has continued to innovate, introducing a number of products and services well ahead of most competitors. These include people greeters, electric carts for less mobile customers, photo services, upscale designer fragrances, a large vegetarian frozen-food section, organic products, and a superior produce department. Operating as a family-owned business has allowed Meijer the luxury of not having to file complex, time-consuming quarterly and annual reports and SEC forms, prospectuses, and proxies, all of which focus attention on current and past performance rather than on long-term strategies to solve consumer problems.

1-800-WE SERVE

Another company that specializes in saving time for its customers is the Hinsdale, Illinois–based ServiceMaster, which in 1996 sold nearly $5 billion of "time" back to its customers by providing a range of services from termite to pest control and on-site furniture repair and residential maid service through its Merry Maids subsidiary.

The 50-year-old ServiceMaster serves over 6.5 million residential and commercial customers through its network of over 5,800 service centers, allowing people to transform chore time into leisure time. No other competitor has a comparable network of services operating under such recognizable brand names as TruGreen-ChemLawn, Terminix, and Merry Maids. Consumers who would rather spend their weekends playing golf and going hiking with the kids than fertilizing their lawns and cleaning their kitchen floors just need to call ServiceMaster. Its customer service number gives away the business—1-800-WE-SERVE. But as in all service businesses, the success of the company depends on the people who work in customers' homes and gardens. Founded on Christian values, the company celebrates the individuality of its employees, yet trains them relentlessly on how to serve. ServiceMaster has put dignity into formerly undignified positions, teaching all employees to honor God in all they do, develop themselves and colleagues through continuing education, pursue excellence, and grow profits. Because the product and concept are sound and the company is well run, ServiceMaster has been cited by the *Wall Street Transcript* as the "most profitable" firm in America in the early 1990s.

REALITY CHECK

In the next century, the realities of consumer resources and consumption behavior will dramatically affect retailing and demand-chain creation among mind-to-market leaders. The imperative to meet the needs and wants of consumers will be greater than ever. This necessity will exist within a consumer landscape defined by a number of factors, including demanding consumers, the growing gap between the haves and the have-nots, the declining middle class, time poverty among the affluent (and to a lesser extent among the rest of society), and the overall increased value of people's time, energy, and attention resources.

Combine these realities with a vastly oversupplied and over-stored marketplace, and the picture comes into focus. An extremely challenging business environment awaits all firms in the next millennium. For some, these realities will spell catastrophe. For those who are able to monitor market realities, population, and lifestyle trends, collect knowledge on each, and transform that knowledge into smart strategic decisions, it will mean success. Opportunities will abound for any firm that is able to operate in this new environment. But in order to meet fully the needs of today's consumers, mind-to-market leaders must first understand the major consumer and demographic trends of our time and those that are emerging for tomorrow.

three

DEMOGRAPHIC TRENDS: A ROAD MAP TO THE FUTURE

"If you don't know where you're going, you may end up someplace else."

— Satchel Paige

DEMOGRAPHICS: MARKET INDICATORS OF TOMORROW

Demographics—the study of population density and distribution as well as the age, education, income, lifestyle, ethnicity, and locale of people—is primary among the indicators that determine emerging market conditions. For managers, strategists, and entrepreneurs, understanding consumers and their consumption patterns—and staying on top of demographic trends—is fundamental to taking control of the demand chain.

Mind-to-market leaders anticipate changes in the following areas and respond to them quickly:

- *Sheer numbers.* To know your future customers, first you must know how many people (or potential customers) there'll be.

- *People's needs and wants.* Age; education; ethnic, racial, and religious identities; and preferences help determine what and how consumers want to buy.

- *Ability to buy.* This encompasses consumers' economic resources, along with their time, energy, and attention "budgets."

- *Willingness to buy.* Here you'll monitor changes in the way consumers make decisions about products, as well as their willingness to take on debt.

- *Authority to buy.* You'll want to determine which members of households and organizations hold the keys of influence and have purchasing responsibility.

While the specifics about consumers change frequently and rapidly, the exercise of gathering and analyzing information should be a constant in any business operation. Without up-to-the-minute data, firms could head in the wrong direction, either targeting the wrong segments or misinterpreting the retail landscape altogether.

Fundamental questions to ask when evaluating consumer information that derives from demographic data include:

- Is this a long-lasting, deep-rooted trend or a passing fad?

- How will this affect my current customer base—both in terms of size and demographic makeup?

- What problems will this trend create for existing products?

- How will my demand-chain partners be affected by the trend?

- What opportunities or problems will it create for my firm as well as my competitors?

- What opportunities will arise from:

  - new product or service opportunities?

  - new positioning of existing product or service?

  - new segments to which to sell existing products?

  - new retail or distribution strategy?

  - the alliance with new demand-chain members?

Nothing beats good market research at identifying trends specific to your firm or industry. But even the largest firms generally combine primary research data—that they've either hired out or conducted in-house—with secondary material collected from such popular trade publications as *American Demographics*. Keeping up to date on current trends by letting other sources do the research for you will give you a lot of bang for the buck, regardless of the size of your company. It is a great tool to help sharpen your instincts in order to guide strategic planning for your company and its demand chains.

If you're an entrepreneur or wish to start a new business, knowing where customers are headed and what they'll be doing, needing, and wanting will help you identify a good niche. If you have a successful, up-and-running business, it's important to keep current in order to effectively steer your company into the future. But no matter what your position, it's always useful to look into the inner sanctums of companies that continue to evolve their businesses and business strategies along with demographic trends to see how they manage to stay on top of the game. You might be surprised how many great firms, like Wal-Mart and Manco, open their doors to entrepreneurs and company officials who are interested in bench-marking or learning how they operate.

A NEIGHBORHOOD GATHERING PLACE

Max & Erma's, a Columbus, Ohio–based chain of 46 restaurants known for its wide-ranging menu, differs from restaurant chains that describe themselves by their specialties (i.e., continental, Italian, or Thai cuisine). Max & Erma's defines its business by the customers it attracts. Indeed, the firm's focus on customer demographics has been a primary ingredient in its recipe for success.

Max & Erma's was started in 1958 as a neighborhood bar (with food on the side) in an ethnic German section of Columbus by Max Visocnik, who together with his wife, Erma Visocnik, ran it for its first 14 years. A cadre of loyal patrons, many of them immigrants from the "old country," worked in nearby factories and breweries and came in regularly to the Cheers-like bar to down Max's beer and devour Erma's famous juicy, oversized hamburgers. Eventually, the small factories departed, taking most of the ethnic German workers with them. In 1972, a small group of entrepreneurs walked into the sleepy bar and envisioned a kind of gathering place that would attract new patrons with gourmet hamburgers and old-world charm.

One of those entrepreneurs, together with several investors, bought out Max & Erma's and initiated a major overhaul. The face-lift introduced a decor of funky antique signs, artifacts, and quirky barstools (which stood on wooden replicas of human legs) and with it a new, down-to-earth menu of gourmet burgers, homemade onion rings, hot apple pie, and build-your-own sundaes. The approach hit exactly the right note in attracting the then-young baby boomers of the 1970s. Soon graduate students, attorneys, businesspeople, and other young professionals who in the next decade would come to be called "yuppies" were flocking to the restaurant, the reputation of which was further burnished by being known as a favorite pickup spot.

Sales boomed, allowing the company to go public in 1982 and open additional restaurants. But by the mid-1980s, as the baby boomers began to mature, marry, and start families, sales sagged, stock prices hit record lows, and some were tempted to write off Max & Erma's as a "has-been."

Pursuing the $25,000 Customer

But, in 1985, the management team, lead by CEO Todd Barnum, decided to rethink the business once again. To that end, it initiated its first major consumer research study. Numbers were crunched and the company realized that frequent customers (that is, those who visited at least three times a month) yielded $25,000 of profit over a lifetime. While most marketing programs emphasize bringing in new customers, management realized that bringing customers *back* was even more important. The point was drilled home to everyone on staff that serving a core customer cold soup or giving him or her bad service did not represent the loss of a $10 meal check, but rather the potential loss of $25,000 lifetime profit. In its goal of *exceeding* the expectations of its core customers, the company initiated several policies to keep 'em coming back. One of the most basic of these should be a requirement for every mind-to-market leader—customer comment cards. Since 1986, every table at Max & Erma's has been stocked with comment cards. Those that are filled out are forwarded directly to Barnum, who tracks the comments, answers some with personal letters, and changes policies in response to a plurality of opinion. For instance, in a 1993 cost-cutting measure, the company replaced its spiced, battered french fries with the plain variety. But consumer consensus was so overwhelming that the company promptly reversed itself and brought back the original recipe.

How does a demand-chain philosophy—with its emphasis on understanding demographic changes and anticipating concomitant consumer needs—affect a restaurant chain such as Max & Erma's?

In the 1970s, its young, university-oriented customers wanted a place to drink beer, eat uncommonly good hamburgers, and ogle the opposite sex. When the yuppies of the 1980s became the muppies (middle-aged, urban professionals) of the 1990s, the restaurant chain continued to reinvent itself to respond to those changes.

Maturing customers and changing norms spelled a decline in the consumption of alcohol and red meat. To become less dependent upon beverage sales, Max & Erma's expanded its menu to include a variety of innovative poultry dishes and such items as veggie burgers and build-your-own chicken sandwiches. While some restaurants added low-fat dishes that were nothing short of character-strengthening, Max & Erma's insisted that all healthful items appeal to customers' palates. Even the menus were written to speak to the ironic sensibilities of the target customer. Low-fat, low-cholesterol offerings were listed under a heading called "When You Want to Be Good." By the mid-1990s, the most popular item on the menu was a tasty, healthful, vegetarian, zucchini-mushroom pasta. With its consumer focus, the company was once again enjoying record sales and continued expansion.

Demand-chain leadership requires firms to respond to various segments of the current market they are attempting to attract on their own terms. For example, the restaurant habits of the so-called

Generation Xers, young people born between the years 1965 and 1979, depart dramatically from older consumers. While baby boomers (born between the years 1946 and 1964) tend to eat in twos and fours and prefer large, comfortable booths, market research shows that Xers like to eat in odd-numbered gangs of threes, nines, and thirteens. What's more, Xers love finger food (like nachos, potato skins, french fries, fried onion rings) and are less concerned than the generation preceding them about its healthfulness. To appeal to the Xers, Max & Erma's designated an area where tables can be moved together to accommodate their flocks (while leaving booths in place for the boomers). To make itself more family-friendly for boomers, Max & Erma's added a video room into the restaurant configuration, thus giving busy professional parents a chance to relax together without the kids for a few minutes before dinner.

Restaurant chains such as Outback Steak House, The Olive Garden, and Don Pablo have also achieved growth with a food focus. But no matter how much diners like a particular restaurant, most don't care to eat Mexican food or steak three nights a week. Thus, those who dine out frequently must seek out restaurants with different cuisines. To draw this customer, Max & Erma's has adopted a "many-menus-in-one" strategy based on consumers' preferences for menu variety. By offering foods ranging from pasta to fajitas, from steaks and salads to chicken quesadillas and vegetarian dishes, Max & Erma's provides something to appeal to each member of the dining party, while bolstering its strategic decision to attract repeat customers.

PEOPLE—THE FOUNDATION OF MARKETS

Population trends on a macro level tell companies how many potential customers to expect in the future. Fertility, death rates, and net immigration affect population figures, making it difficult for business leaders to project reasonably the number of potential consumers at any given point in the future. Trying to stay on top of these ever-emerging numbers requires ongoing monitoring and commitment. To that end, firms must constantly ask questions and aggressively seek answers to seemingly simple demographic questions such as:

- How many people will there be in the future?

- What will the population look like in terms of age distribution, gender, ethnicity, income, employment status, and household makeup?

- How and where will they live?

Of the three significant variables (fertility, death rates, and net immigration), birth rates represent both the most volatile and the most significant statistic. How many babies will be born in the next several years? In the next 25 years? Market leaders forecast the answer by monitoring changes in four variables affecting birth rates. These include:

- Age distribution—the number of women in their childbearing years.

- Family structure—the proportion of people who are married; the percentage of women employed outside of the home; and average age when people get married; as well as the social acceptance of single parenting and nonmarried households.

- Technology—including the availability and cost of contraception and solutions to infertility.

- Social attitudes toward women in the workplace, children, and family.

Forecasting future births is a tricky business, because although the number of couples able to reproduce, *fecundity*, is fairly predictable, *fertility*, the actual reproductive performance, is more difficult to gauge. Therefore, the Census Bureau reports several projections based upon different fertility assumptions: Series I (high) assumes 2.7 children per woman; Series II (middle) assumes 2.1 children; and Series III (lowest) assumes 1.7 children.

Prior to 1993, fertility bottomed out at the level of 1.8 to 1.9 children per woman for about 15 years, but in the early 1990s, it rebounded to almost 2.1 babies per woman. Then, it began to drop once again. Was this short-lived spurt a sign that the American family was destined to grow again in the future? Or was it just a temporary hike? *Boston Globe* columnist Ellen Goodman attributed the surge to the "now-or-never club"—a phrase she coined to mean late births to older women. Assumptions about the cause of the increase make a big difference in projections of future population, as you can see in Figure 3.1.

HOW MANY CONSUMERS?

Since no one knows for sure how many consumers there will be in the future, the best way to make projections for your business is to figure several different scenarios. If fertility rates increase dramatically in the next century, the Census Bureau projects the U.S. population to increase from 262 million in 1995 to 520 million in 2050. I believe fertility rates will remain low, along the lines of the Census Bureau's Series III projections, and that we will see a U.S. population of 268 million in 2000 and 275 million in 2050. It could even be lower.

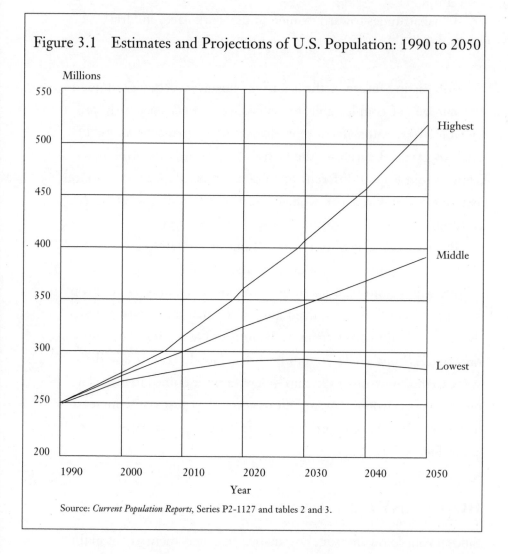

Figure 3.1   Estimates and Projections of U.S. Population: 1990 to 2050

Source: *Current Population Reports*, Series P2-1127 and tables 2 and 3.

As a cautionary example of how rapidly demographic changes come about and how you must work to stay on top of the trends, one need only look at the projections of population decline for the 21st century that came out of 1980s demographic data. Given the falling birth rate of the 1980s, there was real concern among experts that our nation's population would actually *decline* by the year 2050. However, since then, this fear has diminished.

The reason?

People are now living longer. Indeed, overall population levels are projected to be *higher* in the future, primarily because people over age 80 are not dying as quickly as in the past.

And unless some superstork drops a giant new baby boom out of the sky, it appears unlikely that American business will experience much if any expansion from "natural" population growth in the domestic market. This situation is not confined to the United States. In much of Canada, Japan, and Europe, population growth will be slow to nonexistent and in some cases even negative in mainstream, traditional markets. Therefore, the largest retailers and manufacturers must look elsewhere for growth and even survival.

THE "NONEMPLOYED"

Another significant trend that companies will have to confront in the coming years is the continually evolving employment landscape. The trends toward more highly specialized and technical jobs, more service positions, and fewer manufacturing jobs will expand. But we also face perhaps the most dramatic development of all—structural nonemployment.

How many people work determines consumer buying power and impacts businesses of all kinds. While the government reported an unemployment rate of 5.3 percent in December 1996—substantially lower than the average 1986 unemployment rate of 7 percent—unemployment measures assume the common denominator of people seeking employment. They do not account for the many people who do not, or cannot, seek employment. These "nonemployed" are not counted in the unemployment statistics reported on national newscasts. In reality, a whopping 38 percent of all adults over age 18 are *nonemployed*, having no job for which they receive pay.

This nonemployed sector will increase in the 21st century due to several factors: technology and enhanced efficiencies that will eliminate jobs; adults beginning paid employment at a later age; and the increasing number of retirees. (The average retirement age is now 57 and continues to decline—with a little help from corporations who "early-out" workers soon after age 50.)

With labor-intensive manufacturing moving to developing countries, American factories employ fewer workers than in 1950 even though today the factories produce much more. While corporate downsizing may be slowing overall, computer and technology firms continue to invent new ways to accomplish more with less—lower overhead, less equipment, and fewer employees. Indeed, some experts, including Dr. William L. Whittaker, director of the Field Robotics Center at Pittsburgh's Carnegie-Mellon University, now predict that robots will revolutionize the workplace of the first half of the next century as significantly as computers have in the last 20 years.

What all of these converging trends mean to the employment landscape of tomorrow is that there will be more people chasing fewer paid jobs and more looking for alternative work opportunities and income sources. And there will be more "nonemployed" people relying upon savings, the general economy, and potentially unstable government programs like Social Security for their support. The economic and financial strain of providing for nonemployed people will affect the buying power of all of us, and, therefore, the growth potential for all businesses.

FIGHTING FOR CONSUMERS

A sound strategy for growth and enhanced future profitability for mind-to-market leaders is to target population segments that are likely to grow in the future. Due to ignorance, a reluctance to part company with practices that have worked in the past, or the belief that large firms cannot afford to serve small segments, large firms have often in the past neglected many potentially lucrative market segments. These misguided policies provide maneuvering room for small firms who with niche-marketing strategies sometimes succeed in killing giants, segment by segment. Fortunately, demographic information is available to provide some of the knowledge with which to predict the growth segments of the next century.

Among the previously neglected segments that companies must take into account when making their strategic-planning decisions are:

- *Domestic ethnic markets.* Within the United States, growth is occurring in certain segments of the population, most notably the Latino, African American, and Asian populations. Companies that understand how to market effectively to ethnic segments should enjoy growth within these customer segments.

- *Older segments.* Firms must begin to consider marketing to the 65-plus age group. Because not many firms target this category in their traditional market profiles, it represents a highly desirable segment that's "ripe for the plucking."

- *Overseas markets.* Higher birth rates in much of Asia, Latin America, Africa, and parts of eastern Europe make these markets attractive for American and western European companies seeking to expand.

ETHNIC MARKET TRENDS

To understand the magnitude of growing ethnic markets, firms need only analyze birth rates and immigration patterns in the

United States. When today's high fertility rates among ethnic minorities are projected forward, they will yield far more consumers in the future, as seen in Figure 3.2.

What Do the Numbers Say?

Currently about two-thirds of all births in America are non-Hispanic white. However, since this group accounts for such a large proportion of the total population, even a small shift in birth rate produces huge changes in the future. Even using the Census Bureau Series II, midlevel assumptions (rather than low assumptions), white births are expected to fall to 61 percent of total births in 2000, 56 percent in 2010, and 42 percent in 2050. All other racial and ethnic groups will increase their share of births.

Currently, about three-quarters of the population is non-Hispanic white, but this segment is expected to contribute nothing to total population growth after the year 2030. The African American population is projected almost to double from 32 million

Figure 3.2   Projections of the Changing
Ethnic Makeup of U.S. Population

Population Group	Fertility Rate	Projected Percent Change in Population					
		1995– 2000	2000– 2010	2010– 2020	2020– 2030	2030– 2040	2040– 2050
American Indian	2.9	6.6	13.7	13.1	12.1	12.0	11.7
Hispanic origin	2.7	16.3	30.0	26.4	22.6	19.6	17.2
Black	2.5	6.6	12.4	11.9	10.5	9.7	9.4
Asian	2.3	24.5	42.0	31.8	25.6	20.9	17.4
White (non-Hispanic)	1.8	2.0	2.8	2.4	1.1	-0.6	-1.6

in 1992 to 62 million in 2050. After about 2005, more blacks than non-Hispanic whites will be added to the population each year. The Hispanic population is projected to rise from 24 million in 1992 to 88 million in 2050, contributing 33 percent of the nation's growth from 1992 to 2000 and 57 percent of the growth from 2030 to 2050. The Asian and Pacific Islander population is expected to continue to be the fastest-growing group, rising from 9 million in 1992 to 13 million in 2000 and 41 million in 2050. Each year after 2002, this Asian segment will add more people to the population of the United States than will the non-Hispanic white group.

Increases in the size of our total population, including ethnic and racial groups, depend upon birth rates, immigration rates, and the longevity of those currently living. Demographers and strategists examine and project net immigration as a percentage of U.S. population to get a clearer picture of population makeup and to project immigration's impact on future growth. According to the Bureau of the Census, between the years 1941 and 1970, net immigration of people of primarily European descent accounted for about 10 percent of the U.S. population growth. During the 1980s, this number jumped to about 37 percent, and remained fairly high during the years 1991 through 1995 at 28 percent. The early 1990s ushered in the newest wave of immigrants, of whom the largest number were Mexicans; in fact, today, over 45 percent of foreign-born immigrants are of Hispanic origin.

As immigrants become acculturated, they take on a number of characteristics of native-born Americans while retaining many of the cultural attributes of their parents. A Korean American teenager, for instance, might speak Korean at the family dinner table but go to school decked out in a Tommy Hilfiger T-shirt and baggy shorts. Although foreign-born persons account for less than 9 percent of the total U.S. population today, they are growing in numbers and economic buying power. For a glimpse of the future of our entire nation, just visit California, Texas, or south Florida.

Selling to the Ethnic Market

No firm can compete effectively in the 21st century without taking into account the ethnic composition of the market. The days when salespeople said "a customer is a customer is a customer" are over. As in the political process, where ethnic voters can influence—or even throw—an election, the ethnic consumers who "vote" with their pocketbooks can be crucial to the profitability, or even survival, of a business.

Because the days of mass marketing are over, savvy marketers must reach out to increasingly large numbers of segments. Understanding the customs, values, and identifications of various ethnic groups gives insight into how and when customers prefer to shop, what items they'll want to buy, what language they can (or prefer) to read, and which promotions might work best.

Achieving mind-to-market leadership will require strategies based upon knowledge about the minds of ethnic consumers. You must push beyond stereotypes and really study their demographics, habits, and customs to get to know them. For instance, the average age of foreign-born immigrants entering America since 1990 is 26. In a country of aging consumers, this flow of young blood translates into profit opportunities for the discount retailers that flourished in the 1980s. Young immigrants need to buy or rent homes and furnish them for the first time. They are likely to shop at Wal-Mart and Home Depot rather than at fine furniture and department stores.

Unfortunately, the polarization between the "haves" and "have-nots" occurring among native-born Americans also exists among immigrants. While immigrants are more likely than native-born Americans to be college educated, they are also more likely to have never completed high school. The immigrants of the 1980s have now produced a new group of first-generation Americans, a group highly influenced by their immigrant parents. To a greater extent than native-born Americans, foreign-born householdss tend to be multigenerational. It's not unusual for an extended family including children, parents, grandparents, and sometimes aunts and uncles to all live together under the same roof. The Census Bureau's middle series population projections suggest that if children from immigrants born during the next 15 years are added to the number of immigrants entering the United States, they will account for 46 percent of total U.S. population growth to the year 2010. (Bear in mind that the high-fertility projections for Hispanics *could* drop if they become acculturated to mainstream American lifestyles.)

Ethnic-marketing research turns up a wealth of information that should affect your sales and advertising campaigns, as well as the types of products you'll want to offer in many categories. For Latino segments, large-size products and frequent-purchase programs are extremely popular. In the past, companies prospered regardless of the languages displayed on product packaging. Today bilingual packaging is giving way to trilingual (English, Spanish, and French). While it's true that many of these multilingual consumers are capable of reading and speaking English, they feel more favorably disposed toward products on which the language they speak (and dream in) is written.

A number of strategies are currently in place for tapping the growing Latino market. Some companies, like the Secaucus, New Jersey–based Goya, have flourished by targeting the Latino market almost exclusively. Goya reached over $500 million in sales in 1996 through making and selling authentic-tasting Mexican entrées and appetizers to Latino customers, who comprise nearly 90 percent of its customers. The company sells such Latino-kitchen staples as kidney beans, cowpeas, and tootstones (green fried plantains) and delicacies like nopalitos (sliced cactus meat).

Goya's sales have steadily risen over the years. Part of the reason for retailer and consumer loyalty to Goya is its Spanish-speaking sales force, members of whom offer Spanish-owned mom-and-pop stores customized service and significant price breaks like large retailers receive. What's more, the privately held company's product line is deep enough (by 1990, it had over 700 products on the market) that it can offer different selections to please the palates of Latinos from such different countries as Puerto Rico, Venezuela, and Cuba. (In fact, so strong is Goya's penetration of the Latino marketplace that it is now seeking expansion into the *Anglo* market. To that end, in 1995, the company introduced Tropical Blast, a line of tropical juices in flavors such as mango, papaya, guava, and passion fruit that appeal to Anglo tastes.)

Many companies that have in the past appealed to the American consumer in an unsegmented, mass-market fashion are knocking themselves out trying to figure out ways to penetrate ethnic markets. Reacting to the nationwide sellout of a special edition dedicated to slain *tejano* singer Selena in the fall of 1996, *People* magazine recently rolled out *People en Español*, its new Spanish-language edition, which focuses on Latino stars and lifestyles. In four special issues for 1997, *People en Español* hopes to reach a target circulation of about 300,000 readers in selected American cities with sizable Latino populations. Because the magazine is published in Spanish, it will reach new arrivals, not yet fluent in English, as well as bilingual Latino Americans, all of whom are looking for cultural affirmation by reading about Latino personalities who've made successes of themselves in the United States.

Likewise, Banc One is seeing green when it views the enormous Latino market and has jumped on the Selena bandwagon by offering check cards and checks bearing her likeness. This promotion is likely to be a winner given the success other banks have had with similar promotions. The San Francisco–based Bank of America, which marketed special checks featuring art by Asian painter Au Ho-nien during the 1994 Lunar New Year targeted at Asian Americans, enjoyed a sales increase of 85 percent over a similar, nonethnic campaign the year before. And, in what's likely to be an increasingly common occurrence, Banc One has gone so far as to hire a high-level employee with the specialized title of vice president of Hispanic marketing.

Most major companies are likely to follow suit and many already have. Eastman Kodak Co., for instance, targets Latino customers with tie-ins to local cultural events, museum openings, and "family-fun" outings that encourage picture taking with special-guest Hispanic stars, such as Telemundo (Spanish-language television) soap-opera actors. It also supports the California Museum of Latino History, said to be the largest repository of Latino American documents and artifacts in America.

DIVERSITY, AVON STYLE

In attempting to market to different segments both domestically and globally, most companies would be wise to follow in the footsteps of Avon, which in 1996 had net sales of nearly $5 billion and has achieved the distinction of being the world's largest direct-selling company. What makes this cosmetics and personal-care products giant so powerful and effective?

In the United States, the Manhattan-based Avon markets its core cosmetics and fragrance products through 445,000 active representatives who are as varied in their racial and ethnic backgrounds as the products they offer. The company encourages individuals to sell to the community in which they live and with which they identify. For instance, African American sales consultants deal primarily with African American clients. Because they understand the habits, attitudes, experiences, and consumption patterns of the segment to which they sell, these representatives use more appropriate sales techniques and have proven to be more effective. As a result, for many years, the company has enjoyed the reputation as minority-friendly and in 1992 was honored by *Black Enterprise* magazine as one of "The 25 Best Places for Blacks to Work."

Avon's strong base and sales record with ethnic markets in America has given the company an automatic advantage in its expansion into fast-growth markets worldwide. Some of the best new opportunities can be found in Latin America, especially Brazil, Argentina, and Venezuela. Avon is doing well in the Pacific region, notably the Philippines, Thailand, and Malaysia. In South Africa, Avon bought Justine (Pty) Ltd, a well-respected and successful direct seller of beauty products to give it a running start on future expansion into Africa's fast-growing middle class of consumers. It's also expanding in Poland, Russia, and other eastern European markets.

A major reason for Avon's success in diverse markets is its flexibility in product adaptation, as well as its wide range of offerings in a multitude of colors and shades. The company listens to its representatives and carefully tracks consumer trends to formulate its product adaptations for new markets. In its exploding Pacific Rim market, for example, the NeoWhite product was recently introduced to help Asian women even out and lighten skin tones, and it's already become a major hit.

AGING GRACEFULLY

The saying "You're not getting older; you're getting better" summarizes well the current demographic state of the American marketplace. While age no longer defines individuals' lifestyles, it nonetheless provides some guidelines about consumer wants, needs, consumption patterns, and expectations. (However, companies must avoid jumping to dangerous conclusions about consumer wants based strictly on age. Today, consumers are crossing the invisible age boundaries of past generations—behaving and buying differently than their age-group predecessors did.)

Nonetheless, statistics on changing age groups do shed light on growth opportunities for consumer goods. Retailers and manufacturers of consumer products know this. Yet most industrial firms pay little attention to consumer demographics. But mind-to-market leaders, regardless of industry, do—and in order to thrive in the future, others must. The numbers send signals to industrial firms about their customers' potential production and distribution problems. By paying close attention, industrial firms can learn how to best solve their customers' problems and, ultimately, their customers' customers' problems.

Examining how many consumers in each age segment there are and will be in the future helps marketers predict consumer demand and buying trends. In general, the profile of the typical American consumer has changed in the last few decades. The fresh, 30-something face of the affluent yuppie of the 1980s has been replaced in the 1990s by one with more character lines and disposable income. Among younger consumers, only the 20- to 24-year-old age bracket is predicted to grow much in the next decade—good news for retailers like Old Navy and Abercrombie & Fitch, which are effective in reaching this group. The most significant growth by far will occur among the 55- to 65-year-old age bracket, which will reflect the aging of the baby boomers.

THE CONSEQUENCES OF AN OLDER, SLOW-GROWTH CONSUMER BASE

Industrialized countries of the world are seeing dramatic increases in older citizens—the really old. The average age in some European

Figure 3.3   Population Projections by Age: 1995 to 2025
(Numbers in Thousands)

AGE	1995	2000	2010	2025	% Change 1995– 2010	% Change 1995– 2025
Total	262,798	271,237	281,468	290,798	7.10	10.65
<5	19,590	17,943	16,563	16,901	-15.45	-13.73
5-19	56,201	59,298	56,999	53,090	1.42	-5.54
20-24	17,875	17,970	20,320	18,088	13.68	1.19
25-34	40,862	36,741	36,392	38,969	-10.94	-4.63
35-44	42,514	44,364	37,050	38,834	-12.85	-8.66
45-54	31,091	36,840	42,589	33,847	36.98	8.86
55-64	21,136	23,798	34,393	36,821	62.72	74.21
65-Up	33,528	34,284	37,162	54,238	10.84	61.77

Bureau of the Census, *Population Projections of the United States*, Series P25-1130, Low Series, 1995.

countries is even older than in the United States and Canada. Between 1990 and 2000, the population over 90 is projected to increase 50 percent in the European Community and 70 to 80 percent in countries such as Belgium and Germany. Here in the United States, it's estimated that by the year 2050, there will be over 1.2 million people over the age of 100.

What does all of this mean for forward-thinking businesses? Challenges await marketers around the world who must now interpret how these age trends will affect specific products, labor and retirement policies, political elections, family structures, health care, and many other areas of life. They must also gauge the extent of the psychological impact an aging society will have upon others. As younger people are surrounded by older folks, will they realize life could last much longer than it did for generations before them? As a result, will they spend more money on health and appearance products? Or will they save more? Will they spend more time on health-enhancing activities such as bicycling and swimming? Or will they seek out even more pleasure and immediate gratification while they are young? These questions should be posed by your firm, and the answers to them should figure into your strategic planning.

Market researchers already know that baby boomers are listening to their mature-market parents and seeking ways to remain physically and financially fit. They want to live longer and, while they're doing so, enjoy an enhanced quality of life. Their higher proportion of savings also creates a growing market for financial products of many kinds. Companies that appeal to these demonstrated desires should enjoy success in the future.

Worthington Foods, a manufacturer and distributor of vegetarian and other healthy foods, is flourishing because of customers' desire to be healthier. While the company's roots lay deeply embedded in the Seventh-Day Adventist market it was founded to serve in 1939, the "new" Worthington Foods burst onto the mainstream scene with the health consciousness of the 1970s and '80s. Under the guidance of CEO Dale Twomley, sales for the Worthington, Ohio–based company in 1996 reached the $100 million mark, to make it the nation's largest producer of vegetarian foods. Its market is people who believe in good health, good ethics, and good taste, along with customers concerned with preserving the environment and protecting animal rights.

Originally sold only in stores catering to meat-restricting Seventh-Day Adventists, today Worthington Food's healthful products are found in over 96 percent of American supermarkets. Aging baby boomers and older consumers have helped fuel the popularity and sales of the company's Morningstar Farms and Natural Touch brands of vegetarian patties, Spicy Black-Bean Burgers, Garden-Grain Patties, Grillers, Links, egg substitutes, and Ground Meatless. Any company that can find and fill similar niches will have good prospects for future growth.

BEYOND DEMOGRAPHICS

The demographic realities of tomorrow point to a slow-growth, older population base with consumers increasingly in charge. In order to expand under these circumstances, companies must find new segments to target (such as seniors, ethnic customers, and, where possible, worldwide markets).

Slow population growth will place new demands on mind-to-market leaders. In the last century, attracting new customers proved to be a major conduit to success. In the next century, retaining current customers—as the restaurant chain Max & Erma's seeks to do—will be a requirement for staying in business. Firms must connect with consumers early in their lives and keep them coming back. With fewer new consumers available to attract, marketing budgets should be shifted from advertising to customer-service training and consumer research and analysis. Companies will need to understand consumers well enough to have what they want, and to lead or build supply chains that offer customers greater convenience and efficiency. What's more, mind-to-market leaders will need to commit themselves to a program of ongoing change dictated by their customers.

However, in order to penetrate fully the mind of a firm's current or targeted consumers, demographic trends must be coupled with another level of analysis—that is, the analysis of changing consumer lifestyles. To understand fully your customers, you'll need to know their activities, interests, opinions, and values. This information will help to comprise and complete the bedrock of your mind-to-market strategy.

four

CHANGING CONSUMER LIFESTYLES

"If the rate of change inside an organization is less than the rate of change outside, the end is in sight."
—John F. Welch Jr., Chairman
and CEO of General Electric Co.

As crucial as demographics are for getting a handle on what business opportunities will arise in the future, understanding lifestyles, often measured with psychographics—or the study of psychological factors that affect consumer behavior, including people's personalities, motives, interests, activities, and opinions—helps clarify and complete the picture. While consumers in age-based or ethnic population segments certainly share many common characteristics, mind-to-market leaders must take psychographics into account when developing business strategies to appeal to their real and targeted customers. In many cases, lifestyle factors actually *override* age- and ethnic-group characteristics, thus allowing companies to take a more precise measure of the consumers that will ultimately drive their demand chains.

If, for instance, you were trying to determine the buying behavior of a target customer such as Oprah Winfrey, the fact that she's a baby boomer and of African American heritage would be less significant than her wealth, social stature, and lifestyle. However, if you took both her demographic and psychographic characteristics into account, you could come very close to knowing how to reach her, appealing to interests in healthy foods and physical conditioning influenced more by social position than ethnicity.

When getting to know targeted consumer groups, lifestyle information enables you to narrow general market segments, such as baby boomers, into more specialized niches based on preferences, consumer similarities, and the like. By monitoring closely how consumer activities, interests, and opinions (or AIOs) are changing, mind-to-market leaders will be able to tweak the demand chain to better meet the needs of their desired consumers.

To form a psychographic profile of a customer base, researchers collect data from large population samples and interpret it quantitatively. This material is used to best advantage when coupled with data received from such venues as focus groups, in-depth interviews, telephone surveys, and even low-tech methods like comment cards. Quantitative data substantiates trends or ideas, while the "softer" material often provides richer insights and sparks ideas for creative strategy.

LIFESTYLES HAVE GONE TO THE DOGS

One company that has drawn heavily on lifestyle trends to formulate its marketing strategy—and in fact its raison d'être—is PETsMART, the Phoenix-based, mind-to-market leader that has single-handedly created a "big-box" category-killer chain of stores. Founded in 1987, the company has grown the once narrow, commodity-driven product segment of pet food and supplies into the virtually limitless category of everything for most every kind of pet.

Although it achieved more than $1 billion in sales in 1996, PETsMART is trying to carve out an ever-larger piece of the estimated $15 billion pet-product pie.

Looking at the lifestyle characteristics of a typical PETsMART customer, you can see how the company's marketing approach reaches its customers. Had you asked Chris Demos 10 years ago if she would be taking her *dog* to visit Santa Claus at Christmastime, the 32-year-old Pittsburgh accounts manager might have laughed in your face. But today, Demos, who's single and earns over $45,000 a year, stands outside PETsMART with Abbey, an eight-month-old shar-pei, waiting to snap a picture of her pooch perched on St. Nick's lap. The experience does not stop there. Abbey will go on to have a great Christmas, receiving more gifts from Demos's friends and family than some of the "good" children on Santa's list.

Abbey is the light of Demos's life, and while Demos holds out the possibility that someday she'll meet the right man, marry, and have children, she's not going to bank on it. It was during one of her bouts with intense loneliness and longing for connection that she impulsively decided to add Abbey to her life. She's never regretted the decision.

Today, many dogs and cats, like Abbey, act as surrogate children for their owners and surrogate siblings to the owners' biological children. This change in status is reflected in the amount of money spent on them and their role in the household. A generation ago, dogs slept outside the house in doghouses or on tattered blankets on the porch, but today, many cultivate repose on fancy four-postered beds with satin pillows and linens that match the bedding of their owners. Communication between owner and pet is big in the late 1990s, and animal psychologists exist to counsel disturbed pets. But in hearing a number of "pet parents" speak to their four-legged "kids," it is clear that emotional bonding between owner and pet exists. A study done in 1993 confirmed this belief of PETsMART management and shaped the company into what it is today.

Petstyles and Lifestyles

In a recent, highly publicized study, "Bowling Alone: America's Declining Social Capital," Harvard University's Dr. Robert D. Putnam cites declining membership in civic, social, and fraternal organizations—and, yes, even bowling leagues—to make the case that American democracy is imperiled. Americans are living increasingly isolated, work-obsessed, technology-centered lives. In this context, it's only logical to assume that pets could help fill the void left by human relationships that are either unsatisfactory or nonexistent.

PETsMART analyzes demographic and psychographic material to determine how to best sell to its target consumers—young singles, baby boomers, and older affluent customers. When transforming the company from a few retail warehouse firms and evolving its marketing approach, PETsMART management took notice of a number of significant social trends. Perhaps the key factor leading to the elevation of pets in human life has been the trend toward delaying the age of first marriage, which can be attributed to the greater number of years spent in school, increasing financial independence on the part of both sexes, a desire to establish a career before marriage, increased mobility due to job relocation, and increased skepticism about the stability and longevity of the institution of marriage. Regardless of the reasons, men and women are waiting longer to marry, and some are choosing not to marry at all during their reproductive years. This trend leads in part to the previously discussed declining birth rates—especially among non-Hispanic whites. The trail also leads to increase in the ownership of pets.

America's DINKs (dual income, no kids) are quickly becoming DIPs (dual income, pets). Singles and DIPs have the money and affection to lavish on animals—especially when there aren't any children in the present picture. As more time is spent in the office, less time is spent socializing with friends and developing relationships. Singles and childless marrieds arrive home after a long day at work to find their pets eagerly awaiting their arrival.

Pets are popular not only with young professionals but with mature consumers looking for companionship. Whether it be a bird to fill the emotional empty nest, a dog to tag along behind your every step, or a relatively low-maintenance cat to warm a lonely lap, pets help ward off the blues. Research has consistently demonstrated that pets lower blood pressure and add years to the life expectancy of seniors living in nursing homes.

These needs, which factor into the psychographic profile of PETsMART customers, have translated into an upswing in pet ownership over the last five years. According to the American Pet Products Manufacturers Association (APPMA), Americans now own over 236 million dogs, cats, reptiles, birds, fish, and small animals, with 56 percent of all households owning a pet. However, it's interesting to note that 61 percent of all pet-owning households have no children at home.

A Paws-on Approach to Shopping

A large part of the reason for PETsMART's success has been its ability to transform shopping for pets from a chore into an experience of sensory delight, discovery, and camaraderie. PETsMART's objective is for the shopping experience to be a fun outing for owner and pet together. Walk through one of its 280 stores, and you'll hear the clicking of cash registers ringing up a myriad of pet supplies along with the clicking of paws on the store's floor. PETsMART offers shoppers over 12,000 products geared to enhance the lives of not only Fido and Fluffy but lizards, ferrets, fish, potbellied pigs, and snakes.

The new, 40,000-square-foot PETsMART prototype that opened in San Diego in early 1997 is a kind of petly paradise, a Disneyland for dogs and other critters. Divided into seven departments, each is devoted to a specific category of animal. The focal point is a 10,000-square-foot area called All Living Things, positioned at the center of the store. (A similar section is found in every store.) Here, adults and children can learn more about animals and the environment in kiosks equipped with touch-screen computers and mounted displays of books and other information about animals. To appeal to your pet's olfactory senses, the PETsMART bakery wafts the aroma of freshly baked doggy biscuits in the air—a temptation too great for even the most obedient dog. Clustered around the perimeter of the store are specialty services including an obedience-training section, a veterinary-care center, grooming parlors, an animal-nutrition center, and a pet-photo studio.

But no matter how appealing the stores, PETsMART management realized that many of its target customers don't have a lot of time to shop. So in 1996, the company acquired Sporting Dog Specialties, an $84-million-a-year pet and breeder catalog/retailer, as well as State Line Tack, a $50-million-a-year equine supplies catalog/retailer. Through its catalogs, the company now offers an additional 68,000 products to its customers, thus reaching them in locations too small to support a superstore. Combining its catalog mailing list with in-store customer information, the company is able to assemble a formidable database for targeted promotions. (For instance, it could offer a new iguana food to all owners who'd bought in store or through its catalogs in the past 18 months.)

When contrasted with this category's supermarket-aisle sales approach, it's easy to see why PETsMART has been able to dominate and expand the market of these traditional competitors. Most grocery stores sell pet food and a small array of related products, adhering to a strict item/price mentality, but PETsMART offers not only the item but a complete and specialized nutritional program for your pet. The product line is deep and the sales staff is trained to answer questions and dispense advice.

Who would have thought that a company could make billions by selling fish tanks, clothes for dogs, and catnip in enormous stores at the same time that hundreds of small pet stores were struggling for survival? By positioning its brand strongly in the market and doing its homework on consumer lifestyles—figuring out how people's interests in animals and their activities with and opinions about their pets converged—PETsMART built a winner. All firms of any type or size can learn from its market dominance.

KNOWING WHAT CONSUMERS ARE DOING, THINKING, AND BELIEVING

Consumer activities and interests, which often change as people enter different life stages, are relatively easy to monitor by watching what friends, colleagues, neighbors, and communities are doing. For instance, when you see that a growing number of couples are working, it becomes clear that the need for in-home service will increase, thus giving rise to a full-service "service" company like ServiceMaster. People's opinions and beliefs can be a bit more challenging to gauge, however. They require marketers to talk with consumers at length about specific topics such as social issues, politics, business, products, culture, the future, and even themselves.

When firms like Manco and The Limited monitor lifestyles, they look at a wide range of variables in each of the categories shown in Figure 4.1. In order to understand consumers and how best to attract their dollars, firms of all sizes must monitor trends and developments in the areas listed.

All of these categories are influenced directly by an individual's age, income, educational level, and ethnic, racial, and religious beliefs. Consumers also sometimes change their lifestyles depending on their life stages. For instance, as they get older, many people become more conservative in their opinions toward social or political issues. Lifestyles are also directly affected by the values system of an individual. One's concept of what is right or wrong is usually shaped by parents' values as well as peer values. Following the values of a specific consumer segment can help predict what will be important to this group in the future. You can also learn how to appeal to the group emotionally.

Figure 4.1   Categories of Lifestyle Elements

Activities	**Interests**	**Opinion**
work	family	personal
hobbies	home	social issues
social events	job	politics
vacation	community	business
entertainment	recreation	economics
club memberships	fashion	education
community	food	products
shopping	media	future
sports	achievements	culture
computer uses	friends	global issues

CHILDREN AS CONSUMERS

Although the number of young children in the United States is projected to decline in the next few decades, the importance of children as consumers is increasing. Consumer socialization, the process by which young people acquire skills, knowledge, and attitudes relevant to becoming consumers in the marketplace, begins when children shop with parents. Their opinions on brands, types of products, and retailers are formed early on, and these preferences tend to remain strong throughout their lives. Kids' consumer influence is one reason The Gap introduced babyGap, GapKids, and in late 1996 added a kids' version inside the Old Navy stores. Of course, yuppie parents want to buy yuppie-style clothing for their children, but the real advantage for The Gap is the position it achieves in the minds of its future consumers. The Gap hopes that children who wear its fashions when they are young will grow up to buy Gap clothing as adults, just as furniture-chain Ikea hopes that children who play in its in-store play areas while their parents shop for home furnishings likewise will become customers one day.

While children don't sign checks or earn salaries, they do have an enormous influence on spending. On average, children influence 17 percent of family spending in many product categories from cars to vacation purchases, with some categories such as fruit snacks influenced 80 percent of the time by children. By age 10, on average, a child visits stores 270 times per year. According to James McNeal's book *Kids as Customers*, youngsters between the ages of 4 and 12 spend $9 billion per year and influence parents' spending of $75 billion. Among other things, he advises companies to take the time to cater to children—no matter how clumsy or time-consuming these transactions may be. After all, these early retail experiences help to bring children into the fold as customers later in life.

The influence of only children on parents' consumption patterns is disproportionately high. Not only do "onlies" have more say-so over purchasing decisions, but parents who have fewer children on whom to spend money tend to spend more on them. They're likely to pay for designer labels, shop more frequently at specialty stores, and expect more information about products and their usage. What's more, the grandparent market promises to explode further with consumers wanting to buy more and higher quality items for fewer grandchildren. Clothing and educational toys will be important, along with nontraditional gifts such as stocks and property.

Parents want to vacation and spend time with their children, but they also want to spend time alone. In response to this growing trend, Hyatt Hotels and Resorts formed a Camp Hyatt for children between the ages of 3 and 12. The Camp Hyatt Kids Council told the company what's fun besides jumping on beds. Now at most resort-location Hyatts, children can enroll in the program, which costs $5 an hour for supervised fun. Activities include outdoor games, arts and crafts, and sports.

THE UPS AND DOWNS OF TEENS

According to the Bureau of the Census, the number of teens (ages 13 to 19) is projected to increase from about 29 million in 1995 to about 35 million in 2010. And they're armed with money and influence. The Manhattan-based BrainWaves Group recently completed a psychographic study of teenagers, called The New World Teen Study, which revealed that 58 percent of American teens work to earn money.

What do they buy with their hard-earned cash? A lot, and, like their younger brothers and sisters, are major influencers of household purchases. More than half of teenage girls and more than one-third of teenage boys do some family food shopping each week, according to Teenage Research Unlimited. With both parents working, teenagers may be the only family members who have the time to stand in line for products the family needs. What's more, teens influence spending on such products as computers, VCRs, cars, and clothing—often because they know more about them than their parents.

Teens' direct spending often goes to big-ticket items such as vehicles, television sets, VCRs, computers, and music-related products. Since teens have a lot of discretionary money but relatively limited shopping experience, advertising is more important for reaching this age segment than other groups. This is especially true for categories where brand identity is important, such as apparel and shoes. Just ask Nike, Coca-Cola, Airwalk, Oakley, and Abercrombie & Fitch—all considered "cool" brands by teenagers.

Some marketers have been leery of today's teens, stereotyping them as "alienated and unmotivated." They've raised questions about what types of consumers, employees, and citizens this group will turn out to be. But according to The New World Teen Study, teens are far more self-reliant than they are portrayed in the popular media. In fact, 93 percent of American teens believe it is "up to me to get what I want in life" while 77 percent worry about "getting a good job." Mind-to-market leaders must continue to monitor the values and attitudes of this group not only to attract their spending dollars today but to prepare to battle for their patronage tomorrow.

YOUNG ADULTS

Though the 25- through 34-year-old age group is expected to continue to decline in number during the rest of this century and into the next, you'd be unwise to slight this crucially important age group. Traditionally, between the ages of 25 and 34, people form families, have babies, and often buy their first new cars and first homes, and everything to go in them. (Though many consumers are delaying marriage and families, the majority of consumers nonetheless conform to traditional patterns.) They also borrow heavily to finance microwaves, VCRs, electronics, sports and fitness products, and entertainment.

Those at the younger end of this age group and on into their late teens are, much to their dismay, known as Generation X. Raised in the 1970s, this generation was the first to experience the new societal norms of divorced parents, day care, and dual-income families. Their baby-sitters were often television sets, and many today feel most comfortable in front of a screen—whether its a computer screen at work or a TV screen at home. This group is one of the hardest about which to generalize; contrary to the media's depiction, not all are computer nerds, nor do they all have pierced noses. Perhaps the best generalization is to say that they are highly individualistic.

Young adults patronize value-oriented retailers such as Wal-Mart and Target and aren't afraid to buy from dollar stores, discounters, and used-goods retailers, or "remarketers." Xers helped the "vintage" clothing industry flourish while simultaneously sending fad-of-the-moment, full-price retailers like The Merry-Go-Round spinning into Chapter 11. Play It Again Sports and various second-hand ski shops found throughout Colorado are thriving, much to the dismay of Sports Authority, Koenig Sports, independent ski shops, and the now-bankrupt Herman's Sporting Goods. Finding new uses for not-so-new items appeals not only to their frugality and budgets but also to their concerns about the environment.

BABY BOOMERS: FROM YUPPIES TO MUPPIES

Baby boomers, a cohort of 76 million consumers born between the years 1946 and 1964, dominate the minds of marketers today and will continue to do so into the first few decades of the 21st century. With lots of money to spend, they have in the past taught a lesson in excess. But now that the oldest of the group are entering their 50s, they're finding they have too many clothes for their closets, that "stuff" is spilling out of their storage space, and that they own more house than they really need. Though they remain target consumers of the 21st century because of their relative affluence, companies will have to work harder to find merchandise that appeals to them.

The pace of consumption among baby boomers has slowed. Marketers must now strive to reach boomers with quality, durable products. Many in this age segment who have everything will only trade up for the very best and, in some cases, the promise of a product to last a lifetime. Marketers should be aware of a significant group of boomers who've had it with having it all. Frank Levering and Wanda Urbanska speak for many in their generation in their book, *Simple Living: One Couple's Search for a Better Life*. They write not only about trading the fast-paced life in Los Angeles for the slow lane in rural Virginia, but they express the undercurrent of disenchantment with consumerism that could grow into a major force in the next century. Indeed the Trends Research Institute in Rhineback, New York, has identified voluntary simplicity as one of the top 10 trends of the end of this century—one that will continue to grow into the next. Mind-to-market leaders must take this psychographic attitude into consideration by selling thoughtful consumption that is socially and environmentally responsible. Honda and a number of other companies have already co-opted the language of the movement in their advertising urging consumers to "simplify."

A corollary trend is the new migration toward rural and small-town America. In the first six and a half years of the 1990s, 1.8 million net migrants have moved into nonmetropolitan areas—a trend that's expected to continue, due to technology that enables a greater number of people to telecommute from almost anywhere. Baby boomers looking to put down roots are leading the trend. In their book, *Moving to a Small Town: A Guidebook for Moving from Urban to Rural America*, Urbanska and Levering point out that small-town living is not only a demographic trend but represents a "wish fantasy" of our era, displacing the California lifestyle of a generation ago. Though only one in five Americans now lives in rural areas, two out of every three say that they'd live there if they could. Marketers should keep these sentiments in mind when crafting marketing campaigns to target this segment.

What Boomers Want

When they do buy, baby boomers know what they want—quality products that are aesthetically pleasing, personally satisfying, natural, and, if possible, noncaloric. They are experiencing the desire to stay younger and healthier than chronological age had previously dictated, and they are looking for "life-enhancement" qualities in the products they do buy. Particular shoppers, baby boomers purchase from discounters and department stores, from specialty stores or "big-box" stores, or from their home on the television or PC. Mind-to-market leaders must conform their demand channels to meet boomer lifestyles.

In the 20th century, supply chains focused on yuppies because of their discretionary income and their influence on market trends. Stocks of companies that sell services to cater to this age group continue to soar. Most muppies don't need a new car, but if they buy one, it is likely to be higher quality than the last one. Land Rovers, Jeep Cherokees, and GMC Yukons allow baby boomers to haul lots of stuff, put them in touch with the outdoors, and feel as if they are safari-bound with all of the creature comforts this market demands. They may also want a car that will restore some of the "youth" they're not yet ready to concede to the next generation. Automobile advertising targets this age group in commercials such as this one: Driving an Infiniti "gives you the feeling of being young again— without acne."

Appealing to boomer humor and nostalgia are other ways of reaching this market. Old El Paso Salsa uses ads with a plump, middle-aged model for its "nacho" man, taking off on the '70s hit "Macho Man." Cosmetics and personal-care companies are hiring models who speak directly to aging boomers. In a successful campaign, Lancôme signed Isabella Rossellini as its main model and spokesperson in the 1980s—a job she held for many years. Lancôme avoided the mistake some cosmetic companies have made of using 18-year-old models to sell moisturizer and antiwrinkle creams to boomers in their 30s, 40s, and now 50s. In a surprising move, Lancôme "released" Rossellini at age 41, thereby risking the alienation of many of its loyal customers who identified with her.

Many of the eldest of the baby boomers are current (or soon-to-be) empty nesters, that is, in families where the children have not only left home but have also graduated from college. They are often at the height of their careers and earning power, have low or no mortgages on their homes, and have generally reduced family responsibilities and often large amounts of disposable income along with the freedom to spend as they wish. These empty-nested baby boomers frequently indulge in travel, restaurants, and cultural events like the theater.

They watch their waistlines and diets and are good prospects for spas, health clubs, cosmetics, and beauty salons and more healthful foods. As they approach retirement, they tend to purchase upscale condominiums or remodel their homes to feature expanded kitchens and luxurious master baths. They also enjoy eating out. Restaurants such as Max & Erma's, Applebee's, The Cheesecake Factory, and many other competitors are profiting from the frequency with which members of this segment dine out. And more and more, people are opting to take restaurant-prepared food home. According to a Roper poll conducted for a national restaurant group, over half of all 1996 restaurant sales came from home replacement or takeout meals.

THE YOUNG-AGAIN MARKET

A key to understanding the psychographic profile of the generation preceding the baby boom is in its attitude toward youth and aging. In short, they're not willing to give it up—youth, that is. While they may have accumulated chronological age, never make the mistake of calling this rapidly growing segment "old." Today, this 55 through 70-plus group is "young again" in how they think and buy.

Successful marketers focus on this group's cognitive age—the age people perceive themselves to be rather than the age they are. (This thinking also applies to baby boomers.) Understanding how these people feel and act, express their interests, and perceive their looks is useful information when marketing to them. Cognitively younger "older" women, for example, manifest high self-confidence and express greater fashion interests, are more work-oriented, and participate in entertainment and cultural activities more often. In order to appeal to this audience, Duracell ads featured such personalities as Dick Clark, Nolan Ryan, and Bob Hope, who are cognitively young even though they are chronologically old. They represented long, productive lives—features that Duracell batteries possessed as well. These ads also appealed to consumers who, like these stars, still feel young and relate to this group of celebrities.

Like the boomers, older families have more to spend. But their ability to spend doesn't necessarily correspond with their willingness to spend. Many in the "young-again" group are cautious, thrifty consumers because they don't want their money to run out before they do. Marketing "experience" rather than "things" is effective with this age group, most of whom have enough things and in many cases are trying to pare down. The mind of this "young-again" market, therefore, places more emphasis on experiences such as travel, activities (including theater, sports, movies, the arts, and the like), and staying in touch with others.

Experienced shoppers, "young-again" customers are willing to wait to find good value. If given an adequate incentive to do so, they may respond to coupons and be willing to buy at off-peak times. This group focuses on how much they save rather than on how much they spend. Nevertheless, their home mortgages are paid off or nearly so; they have no more college educations to finance; and they have an ample inventory of basic appliances and furnishings. Companies that sell luxury goods, travel-related goods and services, health care, and a wide range of financial services should look at this market and salivate.

Those who are now retiring had the good fortune to live and work during the postwar decades of economic expansion. This gave them a comfortable, even affluent, retirement. On a per-capita, after-tax basis, the average 65- to 69-year-old comes close to having it made. Today and in the future, members of this "young-again" market are averaging higher real income than younger workers, substantially higher cash income, and much higher levels of net worth.

Older consumers are more likely to shop at department or other traditional stores than in discount stores. Socializing may once again become a significant reason to shop, although buying may not be the end goal of the experience. Offering high levels of service will continue to attract this market segment, providing some growth opportunities for companies that saw little expansion in the recent past.

PHYSICAL VULNERABILITY AND NEEDS

Differences in consumption behaviors between older consumers and younger consumers go beyond attitudes. Some differences are based on physical and emotional needs. Eyes don't see as well, creating the need for larger print and bright colors rather than pastels or earth tones. Shiny paper in packaging or print ads gives off an irritating glare that should be avoided. This group finds TV commercials with visual changes every few seconds annoying. A number of changes associated with physical vulnerability and advanced age will create new market opportunities. For example, doorknobs can be replaced with door levers. And demand for push-button phones with larger numbers and volume control will increase.

Three qualities are especially important in products purchased by mature markets: comfort, security, and convenience. Young people may stuff their feet into trendy, high-heeled shoes. Older people want comfort in their clothing, but appearance is also more important to this group than to those of the past, so mind-to-market designers and manufacturers must come up with a way to provide this market with both. They also want greater comfort in their furniture. With institutions handling their assets, the young-again market wants prompt, attentive customer service and good, safe places to park their assets. Young-again consumers also want computers that are easy to operate and understand. They want to go to stores where they're sure they will find what they are looking for at prices they "expect" to pay. And they don't want to struggle with automatic-teller machines and other technology that's too complex to operate.

HOW FASHIONS CHANGE AS CONSUMERS CHANGE

The lifestyle changes that consumers undergo as they age and their circumstances change can dramatically influence the evolution of almost any industry. And the effects of consumer lifestyles on supply chains can only increase in importance and potency as companies allow consumers to drive their futures. Changing lifestyles have influenced the fashion industry: altering the way people dress, what they expect from clothing, and how they value fashion trends.

In 1971, Manny Mashouf opened the doors of bebe in San Francisco, specializing in apparel for the modern, career-oriented woman. Its market niche is classic, durable rather than disposable apparel that women age 20 through 50 can wear to work and out to dinner afterwards. Found in America's best malls, bebe competes head-to-head with such big names as Nordstrom and Saks Fifth Avenue for consumers' mind-space. Today, 79 stores strong, bebe turns the heads of consumers and other retailers alike.

Why all the fuss? It sells clothing to a well-defined market segment, often at a sales rate of $1,000 per square foot, and enjoys a sales turnover several times that of most of its competitors. The chain plans to add five new stores by mid-1997, while other small- and medium-size chains are closing their doors, singing the hard-times-in-apparel blues.

To understand what's driving bebe's success, it is first necessary to examine what fashion is. Designers and merchants might turn to the runways of Paris and New York for the answer. Others might look to Hollywood stars. From a marketing perspective, fashion is a statistical concept, referring to what the majority of consumers are buying. For some, fashion is a risk reducer. Consumers—especially young ones—rely on fashion to reduce the risk of dressing "wrong," which could result in social embarrassment. Even though they may not look their best in some of the latest fashions, they increase their confidence by wearing what their peers deem "the right" look.

Bell-bottoms, hip huggers, crepe skirts—some call them fashions, others call them fads. What they are are *disposable fashions*. Such items live short lives in consumers' closets, usually only one or two years. Then, it's out with the old and in with the new. Disposable fashions appeal to younger consumers, who shop for leisure but don't have as much money to spend on apparel as older buyers. These items must be priced lower, often at the sacrifice of quality—a trade-off young consumers are willing to make.

During the 1990s, as the all-important baby boomers aged, the market for fashion evolved. Consumers had matured and looked for ways to express their individuality. Durable fashions experienced a surge in popularity. They can be worn for a number of years, allowing consumers to expand their "collections" each year. On average, mature consumers have more money but less time to spend on clothing. Yet they expect their purchases to coordinate well with what's already in their closets, creating a composite wardrobe based on style or a particular mode of expression. For the upscale customer segment, apparel represents an investment of scarce resources from time, money, attention, and energy budgets. And consumers expect a good return on their investments.

THE BEBE DIFFERENCE

Bebe markets style—a look or creative approach to dressing that's consistent from year to year. Of course, it sells some fashion apparel that changes to reflect current trends, giving it a chic, up-to-date look. It pioneered the "Amanda" look (with short skirts and fitted jackets in pastels and bold, eye-catching colors) on the hit TV show *Melrose Place*, but its core merchandise consists of classics that appear in identical colors, fabrics, and textures for a minimum of three years.

Bebe's current designs incorporate timeless quality and style with the latest trends to enable customers to build a wardrobe piece by piece. Even with seasonal changes in style and color, the bebe look is consistent—clean and modern, with a focus on helping clients build wardrobes that last. For example, the same shade of black is maintained in core fabrications from season to season. Bebe may introduce a new black blazer to the line, but shoppers know it will coordinate and match the black items purchased the previous season.

Bebe's customers are primarily mid- to upper-level executives from CEOs and lawyers to assistants and secretaries. They share enough fashion concerns and characteristics to constitute a market segment. The executive market believes people who succeed dress to the highest position they hope to attain. Many secretaries need to look as good as the executives they work with and the corporate guests they meet. Both segments constitute bebe customers. But these segments differ in their resource constraints (both time and money) and lifestyles, which creates different *buying styles*. Executives and attorneys have the money to buy several complete outfits at bebe and update them each year. They buy more items at a time but visit the store less frequently because of time constraints. Assistants and junior executives can't always afford to buy a complete outfit, but they may invest in a blazer one year and skirt and slacks the next.

Both groups of bebe customers lead hectic lifestyles, creating the need for versatility in their apparel. Because they need to dress for a variety of activities—business meetings, weekend get-togethers, travel, and evening events—they like the option of wearing a suit to work and then wearing the suit jacket with casual slacks for a relaxed social gathering.

Bebe has monitored how lifestyles affect how customers buy apparel, what attributes they look for in fabrics and styling, and how they mix and match their clothing to create new looks. Through astute observation, bebe has evolved into a style-oriented retailer whose growth is fueled by changes in the market.

MONITORING CONSUMERS FOR CONTINUAL IMPROVEMENT

When workers in all areas of an organization share a common vision of markets and consumption patterns of the future, they are better equipped to change the firm and themselves, to improve continually.

Why? Because they constantly focus on questions such as, what will people buy in the future? What segments of the market will become more important in the future? Which segments will decrease in their profit potential?

Mind-to-market leaders possess the ability to change not only themselves but the entire supply chain to fit the needs of the market. These leaders generally program their organizational structure and methods of operation for continual improvement—gradual change in strategies and tactics closely related to changes in the market.

There are very few secrets of success in business, just the degree of mastering them. Firms like Manco and Kinko's practice one key element each day—keeping both eyes and ears on the minds and consumption patterns of consumers to identify ways to develop new products and services, and, more importantly, to improve what already exists. If you listen, the market will tell you what must be done to achieve continual improvement.

Businesses and organizations of all sizes can monitor changes among consumers just as many mind-to-market leaders do. Any firm can track the categories in Figure 4.1 by talking to consumers either in formal settings, like focus groups or in-depth interviews, or informal settings, such as at social or volunteer events. For example, each year I volunteer at a Marshall Field's charity gift wrap to benefit the Directions for Youth agency in Columbus, Ohio. I take this time to talk to shoppers, other volunteers, and store personnel to get a feel for what consumers are buying, how much they are spending, how they feel about shopping, and their moods in general. Of course, you can't overgeneralize about the masses from isolated input like this, but you can formulate ideas to explore further with quantitative or secondary research.

When conducting lifestyle assessments, focus on changes that could directly impact the future of your business. As you examine the different psychographic categories, you'll want to probe the following areas for trends in each category, asking questions along the lines of:

- Work—How much time is spent at work? What types of problems arise from work-related activities? How do people get to and from work?

- Hobbies—How are various hobbies (crafts, for example) increasing in popularity among which consumer segments? Why?

- Social events—How much time and importance are consumers placing on social gatherings and what types?

Monitoring other lifestyle patterns such as how people entertain themselves (and others), shop, exercise, and promote healthful lifestyles helps get inside the minds of consumers. Some questions to ask when monitoring these activities include:

- How has this activity increased or decreased in popularity in recent years? Why?

- If consumers are spending more time on a new activity, what are they spending less time doing?

- How much is the average consumer spending in terms of money, time, and attention on this activity? Do you believe this will increase or decrease?

- What consumer needs or problems are created by this activity?

- Can you attribute increases in sales of a specific product line to this lifestyle trend?

- How can you address these changes in opinions and interests in communication pieces, such as advertising?

- What types of new products or services could further foster a consumer's interest in a specific topic or activity?

In examining consumers' psychographic portraits, be sure to define which consumers (in terms of age segment, ethnicity, income level, and education level) are participating in and driving these trends. This will help you understand the impact of a lifestyle trend on overall market demand and on demand for your company's existing products.

Industrial demand chain leaders also need to follow consumer trends because they will ultimately affect all of their customers and channel members. The worksheets shown in Figure 4.2 provide a skeleton of how business-to-business firms and consumer-product firms alike can monitor trends and anticipate market opportunities for themselves and their customers.

Monitoring consumer demographics and lifestyles goes hand in

glove with building demand chains. Sometimes we watch the formation of change firsthand, while at other times, we read about
them. Regardless, mind-to-market leaders use this information to
formulate strategies allowing their demand chains to capitalize on
these newly identified opportunities.

Once you've gained a full-bodied idea of what consumers are
like based on combining demographic and psychographic information, you will own a knowledge base on which to build the demand
chain for your company.

Figure 4.2   Consumer Trend Analysis Worksheet

Industry:_____

Trend	Who Affected My Trend (Current Customers, Competitors, etc.)?	How Will Trend Affect Our Company?	Effect on Existing Products/ Services	Opportunities For New Products/ Services	How Will this Change the Way We Do Business?	Are Competitors Poised to Take Advantage of this Trend?	Which Partners in the Chain Can Help Us and How?

---

five

FUELING DEMAND CHAINS WITH KNOWLEDGE

"Most people skate to where the puck is. I try to skate to where the puck will be."

—WAYNE GRETSKY

Paul Orfalea is the Wayne Gretsky of retailers. His name may not be emblazoned on the jerseys of aspiring young entrepreneurs, but his Gretsky-like marketing moves win fans of all ages every day. Practically every household in the United States and Canada recognizes or uses his office supplies and services. They buy directly from him at one of his 800-plus stores. Or they buy from one of over 200,000 businesses that use his firm to help operate their businesses. Paul's place—open 24 hours a day year-round—is "the new way to office" for entrepreneurs of every size and millions of consumers.

When Paul Orfalea was growing up, everyone called him Kinko because of his kinky red hair. Today, everyone calls his company by the same name—Kinko's. Kinko's is a prime example of a company that has understood demographic and psychographic changes in the marketplace and put this knowledge to work in building the strategy and the company. In fact, to a larger extent than in the vast majority of firms (and certainly most of its competitors), Kinko's has turned its knowledge of the consumer and the marketplace into a driving force behind its success.

Though Kinko's copy centers mastered the two fundamentals of the marketing mix—offering a good product at a fair price—Orfalea recognized early on that product and price were not enough to win the market. After all, his rivals could quickly follow suit. Ploys that essentially one-up the competition may be effective in the short term, and they may be effective in small markets, but in large markets and over the long haul, winning strategies must focus not only on state-of-the-art product improvement and best price but also on new or improved forms of supplying those products and services to consumers.

How mind-to-market leaders gain knowledge about ways to better supply consumers and how they act upon that knowledge is what distinguishes the winners from the also-rans. Their success lies in obtaining and processing the knowledge required to create comprehensive strategies for seizing command of demand chains.

Indeed, thorough knowledge of the market and its dynamics can help businesspeople identify new opportunities. Core elements of this knowledge include:

- Consumer markets—how the market for products and services is changing via trends in economics, demographics, lifestyles, resources, values, and ethnicity.

- Consumer behavior—analyzing the activities involved around purchasing, consuming, and disposing of products and services; the decision processes that precede and follow purchases; and the consumption patterns that emerge.

- Technology—identifying changes in technology that affect the way consumers buy, receive, and consume products and services.

- Logistics—or how to get the right product to the right market, at the right time, in the right condition, at the right price.

Understanding these core areas and watching closely for changes within them provides the knowledge base for devising new product and distribution strategies and improving existing ones. If an entrepreneur or company leader understands why and how people like to buy—as Orfalea does—then that person can persuade customers to buy more. Mastering these areas also guides a company's strategic planning process. For example, technology determines what can be offered to the marketplace and how it can best be distributed, but consumers determine what products will be accepted and how they will be bought. With a combination of knowledge bases, firms are better able to develop visionary strategies based on the realities of the market to propel them safely and successfully into the marketplace of the 21st century.

OF COPIERS AND CUSTOMERS

Paul Orfalea was already a keen observer of consumer behavior while an undergraduate student of finance at the University of Southern California. Though he graduated with a C average, Orfalea came up with what would prove to be a brilliant business concept: providing convenient, low-cost copy service for students near university campuses. In 1970, Orfalea got a $5,000 loan and opened his first Kinko's shop in a former hamburger stand—not at USC where he was studying and living but near the University of California at Santa Barbara campus where he planned to make his home after his graduation the following year. The first space he rented was so small that he had to wheel the copier machine out to the sidewalk to make copies—an economic move that providentially helped draw attention to his fledgling business.

However, modest beginnings didn't impede rapid expansion. By the end of the decade, Kinko's had 80 stores, located primarily near universities on the West Coast, and was providing such sidelines as custom publishing materials for college classes (popular with professors who could create individualized, supplemental reading packets that could be photocopied and easily changed each semester).

Though it was clear that Orfalea had created a winning formula, he exhibited a key characteristic of mind-to-market leaders—the drive to refine continuously his knowledge about customer wants and to expand his offerings to meet those needs. To that end, he paid special attention to feedback from the dissatisfied customers of his competitors. Early on, Orfalea observed that students were often desperate to photocopy their papers in the wee hours of the night (when they finished writing them) at a time when ma-and-pa print/copy shops were closed. While college libraries usually stayed open longer than the independents, they sold poor-quality copies at steep prices (often as much as 10 cents a page).

Kinko's filled the gap by offering sharp copies at low prices (4 cents a page at his first shop) during student-friendly hours. While Orfalea may have lacked the normal prerequisites for entrepreneurship—start-up capital and a formally structured organization—his insight into consumer demand was so vital and on target that it propelled him to create, obtain, and grow both the capital and organization.

Kinko's initially focused on student markets, and to this day you'd be hard-pressed to find a major university campus without a Kinko's nearby. But because Orfalea kept his customer research current and studied demographic and lifestyle trends, he was able to foresee an important development that would dramatically impact the expansion of his business—it was the emergence in the 1980s of the home office. The home-office boom was fueled in part by corporate downsizing but also by the entrepreneurial spirit of the post-hippie era. Many start-up entrepreneurs established offices outside the home, but no matter where they hung their shingles, both types of small-business people needed convenient, inexpensive access to copiers as well as the ability to generate brochures, proposals, and reports in order for their businesses to compete.

MASTERING THE STUDY OF CONSUMER BEHAVIOR

The focus of Kinko's competitors (Sir Speedy and Pip Printing are the best known) was on production via specialized equipment and processes, such as copiers and offset printing. But by the early 1980s, Orfalea understood the consumption patterns of his market well enough to know that students and professors were relying more heavily on computers to create and produce professional-looking documents. So, in 1984, the company added computer workstations with high-resolution printers, many of them color, for enhancing and completing documents.

Kinko's marketing department also recognized that with these specialized, higher-tech applications and offerings, customers would need additional assistance. So the company implemented a technical-support training program to enable the entire staff to answer questions. As a result, Kinko's employees—or "coworkers" as they're called—have the expertise to help customers use specialized equipment and answer all their technical questions. Kinko's approach to customer service is more fine-tuned and comprehensive in scope than its competitors', which focused solely on buyer behavior. Indeed the company has long focused on *consumption* behavior: how and why people buy and use products, including the decisions they make before and after money changes hands.

In addition to investing in state-of-the-art equipment and employee expertise, Kinko's responded to another basic customer need. Frequently, when copying papers, customers would come up short or empty-handed supplywise. In phases, the company introduced a wide array of complementary merchandise—basic office supplies such as paper stocks, report binders, and presentation materials. And it began stocking the shops with staplers, glues, collators, and hole punchers for customers to use free of charge while in the store. Part of Kinko's strategy was for customers to see it as a one-stop shop for document production. To that end, products are priced competitively rather than at "resort" or "airport" rates (which would encourage customers to buy elsewhere except in a jam). By responding to, and anticipating, consumer needs, Kinko's created its own demand chain.

THE NEW WAY TO OFFICE

By 1989, Kinko's began to shift not only its focus but its positioning to zero in on its small-business and home-office target market. Then the world's largest retail provider of document copying and business services, in the early 1990s, Kinko's introduced an advertising campaign to buttress its new positioning. Ads for Kinko's, billing it as "Your Branch Office," began to appear on national television. In 1996, the company slogan was refined as "The New Way to Office." Today, the average store occupies over 7,000 square feet (up from 1,500 square feet just a decade earlier)—in part to accommodate a dramatically inflated retail inventory of office supplies. In addition to giving the documents of small-business customers the professional "edge," Kinko's provides special touches, such as soft or hard binding, and Velo and thermal tape binding. It also helps create effective direct-mail pieces for individuals and firms of all sizes and offers resources for double-side copying, perforating, and labeling.

By keeping abreast of the emerging needs of its small-business customers as well as the cost-saving trends in larger corporations, Kinko's has tailored its services and grown its business to meet these needs. For instance, as many larger corporations began experimenting with videoconferencing to reduce travel costs, Kinko's jumped into the fray, offering a similar service to firms without the capital for such equipment or the expertise to run it. By shifting capital costs from its customers to itself, Kinko's in effect reduced overhead for its small-business customers, thus creating a new niche business.

IT TAKES A VILLAGE

A major source of knowledge for Kinko's innovations comes from those people closest to the customer, the coworkers. Kinko's self-styled "village" culture—it consists of 23,000 coworkers and stresses teamwork, open communication, and the primacy of employees' personal and professional needs—helps foster a spirit of camaraderie and teamwork among staffers in which communication is encouraged. Suggestions are welcome year-round, which come to company headquarters in the form of letters, E-mail messages, and direct communication between store managers and corporate headquarters. While in the past, the coworker who submitted the single best idea over the course of a year won a vacation trip to either Disney World or Disneyland for himself or herself and all of his or her coworkers, the award trip was recently changed to honor the most profitable store in the chain. During that extended weekend—in what has become an annual exercise in hands-on, mind-to-market leadership—Orfalea, company vice presidents, and the board of directors act as regular retail coworkers, assisting customers on the copiers and other machines and ringing up sales at the cash registers.

KNOWLEDGE OF THE TOTAL CONSUMPTION EXPERIENCE—THE STRATEGIC ASSET

Firms with technology, capital, and property are losing out to firms with knowledge of the consumer—and a readiness to act on it. While it does not appear on the balance sheet, knowledge will ultimately affect the bottom line of all firms in the new millennium.

Skeptics circa 1970 might have dismissed Paul Orfalea's chances for success. After all, in the early years of his company, campus bookstores and libraries had locational advantages, and many print shops and office supply stores had national franchise visibility. But, in a few short years, these competitors lost their competitive market share to Kinko's. While they narrowly focused on individual products, services, and price, Kinko's focused on users' *total consumption experience*. This allowed Kinko's to create a channel of distribution based on demand rather than supply. Kinko's knowledge was an asset of greater strategic value than the money and buildings listed on its competitors' balance sheets. As Kinko's knowledge base expands and evolves (as new competitors such as Staples and Office Depot enter the field), the firm will continue to reinvent itself.

Indeed, in the home-office and communication products industry, Kinko's copied no one, but the company's formula for success *can* be duplicated:

- Find a market niche not being served satisfactorily by existing firms.

- Build the organization around what consumers need.

- Provide services in the store to help them solve problems.

- Monitor changes in consumers and in the marketplace.

- Develop strategies to take advantage of the changes and expand offerings and services accordingly.

- Implement changes more quickly and effectively than competitors.

- Foster an entrepreneurial, family-like corporate culture among employees at all levels throughout the corporation.

Paul Orfalea wrote the book on applying knowledge from the mind of the market to his company and its demand chain. As a mind-to-market leader, Kinko's has positioned itself for growth in the next century—on a global platform with stores now in Japan and Korea.

KNOWLEDGE IN DEMAND CHAINS

Knowledge fuels demand chains by directly influencing the decisions and strategies of the demand-chain organizations. Extracted from consumers in the marketplace, knowledge flows to demand-chain members who analyze the information and share it amongst themselves. But knowledge is not a product, it's a process, providing an ever-changing stream of information about what to produce and how to market, distribute, and sell it best.

The knowledge "process" has become so valuable that in an era where content is king, having access to knowledge and having the ability to control and manipulate it is quickly becoming the most valuable of all commodities. Bill Gates has become the richest person in America, in part because he now dominates the information demand chain. Any banker will also tell you Gates is the most feared person in the financial services industry. As evidence of this sentiment, a group of bankers and other financial executives successfully lobbied the U.S. Justice Department to prevent Microsoft from purchasing Intuit, a leader in developing financial software for consumers. And leaders of the conventional financial industry also maneuvered to limit Microsoft's entry to on-line computerized information services.

What they feared was not the expansion of Gates's fortune but his control of the tools that provide access to knowledge and information. The key to the man's wealth, power, and respect lies in his control of information, which, when manipulated, becomes knowledge—Microsoft's strategic asset. Microsoft holds the keys to the control board of the information supply chain, not only in banking but in many other areas of business and consumer relationships.

Since Microsoft already dominates the software necessary for information transfer, is it fair to say it also controls access to consumers' minds? In a sense it does through customers' computers, where they store financial, personal, and other information. Banks can still be banks and brokerage firms can still be brokerage firms, but the firms that control electronic access to the supply chain have the potential of leading the entire financial industry. The organization that controls the demand chain probably does not want to own, operate, or even control many of the rest of the organizations—just the most profitable ones!

A 1991 article, "The Computerless Computer Company," appearing in the *Harvard Business Review* accurately predicted that computer firms that made no computers would be more valuable than companies that made the "boxes." At the time it appeared, people scoffed. But they'd stopped laughing three years later when the increasing value of Microsoft stock crossed the trajectory of the decreasing value of IBM stock, thus surpassing it. Much of IBM's recent resurrection in its stock value is related to consulting services, systems, and software rather than the archaic manufacturing of the actual units.

Many observers believe IBM stock will never regain its former standing based on its ability to make either mainframes or PCs. But when IBM again begins to affect dramatically thinking about information technology and business strategy, it can begin to control the computer supply chain. Indeed, the company's new marketing strategy is based upon demand-chain leadership rather than manufacturing and design—an approach that already seems to have paid off with business buyers (though less so among personal computer users in the "click-and-drag" generation). IBM is recovering, but its future ability to be a demand-chain leader will depend on its ability to acquire and harness knowledge and its responsiveness to what it learns.

Indeed, the difficulties of Apple Computer Inc.—possibly our country's preeminent personal computer designer and innovator—can be traced to its adherence to obsolete channels of distribution (namely its insistence on selling through dealers rather than going to mail-order sales, as compared to Dell or Compaq, which pioneered innovative distribution channels that cut costs significantly and reached out to a broader base of buyers). Apple is a case in point that regardless of how superior a product may be, and Apple users are among the most zealous, if a firm remains clueless about *how* consumers want to buy, that company will be relegated to low profitability, a struggle for survival, and perhaps even partnership with an entity that has greater power in the distribution channel.

MICROCENTER, CHANGE MASTER

One company that has been adept at delving into consumer minds and delivering products into their hands is MicroCenter.

MicroCenter, a privately owned computer sales and service company, used superior service to gain a competitive foothold in a new industry and create its own demand chain. To this day, service has provided differential advantage for the company, which now has 11 locations in Ohio, Georgia, Pennsylvania, Massachusetts, California, Texas, and Washington, D.C.

The company started in 1980 in a vacant variety store in an Arlington, Ohio, mall. From the ashes of a dying retail category arose a mind-to-market leader in the exploding computer business. With annual sales in 1996 approaching $1 billion, the company thrives because of its ability to act upon knowledge about retail and business consumers as well as to respond to innovations in technology and distribution methods.

While, for example, most computer retailers in the early '80s built stores and kept their layouts essentially unchanged until forced to modify them, MicroCenter changed the store—sometimes every day. Cofounder John Baker took daily store walk-throughs, mulling over how products, fixtures, or displays could be better positioned to meet consumer needs and attract their attention. As a result, his store walk-throughs became store "change-throughs." If an employee would argue that a certain display or configuration had just been set up, Baker would simply say: "Change it again."

The changes Baker made at MicroCenter were based on a combination of his good instincts and on knowledge gleaned from the company service center where customers would bring in their problem computers and voice their complaints and wishes. By paying close attention to customer feedback (supplemented by keeping up with demographic and psychographic research), the company introduced a number of new services. In the early days of computers (but also up until the present day), business buyers required training. MicroCenter expanded rapidly, adding skilled teachers and taking over many of the adjacent shopping center vacancies for classrooms. (When selling in quantities to businesses, for example, MicroCenter would figure in the cost of in-store training.)

After buying computer equipment, consumers invariably needed service—a weakness of many computer retailers. MicroCenter dedicated an entire area of the store to servicing computers, providing the same level of repair and consultation for individual customers as it did for big-business customers. (The service department outdistanced its competitors by offering such features as on-the-spot estimates and its willingness to repair every brand of computer—not just items purchased in house.) What's more, in the early days, the firm was unusual in that it sold both IBM and Apple products; it eventually enlarged its facility to include ministores devoted to each company.

By getting to know its customers, MicroCenter was better able to sell to them. When a customer came into the store, for instance, a salesperson would quiz him or her about what he or she would be using the computer for. If a novice wanted to write a political thriller, for instance, she might be steered toward a user-friendly Macintosh; if the customer intended to take work home from his IBM-equipped office, an IBM-PC might be recommended. When its sales force ventured outside the store to sell to big businesses and government agencies, its competitive advantage was in being able to offer service contracts and customer training along with the hardware and software. By establishing itself as a "value-added reseller," MicroCenter was able to sell hundreds of computers at a time, putting the company in direct competition with manufacturers and fattening its bottom line.

Direct mail changed the scope of the company's business and pointed it in new directions. In the early 1980s, when large hard drives on personal computers were rare, consumers consistently complained of inadequate data storage space on floppy discs.

MicroCenter seized upon the diskette market as a sales line and revenue enhancer. While most retailers simply mark up and resell what they're offered by manufacturers, in this case, MicroCenter decided to go to the source and procure its own supply. The company sent buyers to the Far East to obtain floppy discs directly from manufacturers to sell directly to its customers—first in its stores and later by mail. Supply-chain efficiencies and lower packaging costs allowed MicroCenter to sell floppy discs for 19 cents apiece in quantity purchases compared to competitors' prices of 59 cents or more each. The strategy worked so well that in 1985 MicroCenter was selling discs in larger quantities than IBM. By passing savings on to its customers, the MicroCenter brand gained even more credibility. Its success with the floppies gave MicroCenter two assets: a large mailing list of dedicated customers and knowledge about reliable supply-chain partners for the computer accessories business, along with the logistics capability needed to create a demand chain that could expand beyond computer supplies.

Based on its newfound knowledge, MicroCenter integrated manufacturing, retailing, and multiple channels of distribution—a revolution in the computer business—to create its own laptop computer called the Winbook, which was introduced in the spring of 1993. The product's development, which began in 1992, was based on extensive marketing research and analysis of competitive brands.

How can a retailer be effective in developing such a technical product? A retailer who talks to consumers every day, handles their hardware, software, and implementation problems in its service department, keeps systematic records, relays this information to its consulting department (which is itself focused on developing products and services to meet future needs), and understands their price sensitivities and brand and feature preferences knows its consumers extremely well. Getting market knowledge directly from consumers gave, and continues to give, MicroCenter an edge over manufacturers who obtain such information secondhand.

When MicroCenter decided to venture into production, it tapped high-quality Korean manufacturers for the job. Made up of quality components including Intel's Pentium-brand chip, the Winbook was created for the MicroCenter market. The result? *PC Magazine* and others rated it as the "best laptop computer in its class."

By creating and responding to its own demand chain, MicroCenter found success in the cutthroat computer market.

Its strategies included:

- Living by continual, knowledge-based change. When your company gets something right, go to work to figure out how to make it better.

- Using direct mail to break into national and international markets, particularly when competitors confine themselves to regional boundaries.

- Integrating the supply-chain functions of manufacturing and retailing.

These strategies apply no matter what your industry. MicroCenter applied practical strategies to the computer industry and carved out a lucrative niche for itself, offering a recipe for turning a small retail business into a billion-dollar firm.

THE FORD TAURUS: AN EXERCISE IN TEAMWORK

Consumers have reasons for everything they do. The problem is that most managers do not take the time or the trouble to understand those reasons. But maps that show why people buy are available to anyone who takes the time to ask the right questions and to listen to the answers. When it comes to consumer behavior, the question always facing managers is: How do I understand how psychology, sociology, economics, and anthropology relate to the mind of the market?

When traditional companies step beyond old paradigms—when they drop the old, bureaucratic, and often insular in-house framework and just stop to listen to consumers—they will inevitably stumble onto the path of success.

In 1985, the Ford Motor Company did precisely this. Taking the bold step of trying to create a world-class automobile, it formed a special team to make this happen. Because automobile price and reliability were comparable among the major American manufacturers, Team Taurus focused its attention on an idea—novel among Detroit automakers—of pleasing the customer.

Composed of 60 members from marketing, engineering, design, and finance, Team Taurus conducted research to learn exactly how people use cars and what they want in an automobile. Forty-five hundred consumers were quizzed about specific feature preferences and driving considerations, and the team studied every facet of their interactions with the car. Among other things, it learned that consumers wanted easy access to such controls as seat and mirror adjustment knobs and an easy-to-find gas-tank release.

The team also closely studied competitors' models, evaluating every major competitor in terms of 400 separate components, features, and functions. The idea was not to rate every competitive car as a whole but to evaluate each of the features and to single out the best-in-class, or BIC, among them.

The team's findings directly influenced the car's design. The cockpit was designed to bring the instruments and control systems within quick and easy reach of the driver, creating driving safety and comfort. The ergonomic seats were easily adjusted and better fit the needs of both drivers and passengers, while dual sun visors shaded the sun at any angle; backlit controls made for easy visibility at night, and a map light gave clear view to the front-seat passenger while not casting glare on the driver's eyes. The practical benefits of the Taurus's aerospace design included reduced wind resistance and drag, better gas mileage, and enhanced handling.

When the Taurus was introduced in December 1985, it met the target on 320 of the 400 selected BIC features, matching or improving upon a full 80 percent of the best features found on the best cars of its class in the world. While the Taurus equaled competitors on styling, price, and other "salient" (or primary) criteria, it exceeded its competitors on many of the less important attributes, which became "determinant" (or determining) attributes.

Though the car initially met with only modest success, by 1986, the Taurus had become such a hit that Ford beat Chevrolet in overall automobile sales for the first time in nearly half a century. By 1995, Taurus had dislodged the Honda Accord for two consecutive years as the number-one-selling car in America. Ford's exercise in delving into the mind of the consumer delivered an overwhelming victory for the company, winning it the gold medal in the ever-competitive mind-to-market race.

Altering the Alternative

In anticipation of the 1996 model year, Team Taurus went back to work to update and redesign its star performer. After 38 months of work, in the fall of 1995, a new Taurus rolled off the production line. The car made its debut in an environment vastly changed from a decade earlier. More consumers were buying minivans and sport-utility vehicles over sedans. And in the midsize, passenger-sedan category, Honda Accord and Toyota Camry were competing fender to fender with the Taurus.

In developing the updated model, Team Taurus had gone back to the drawing board, once again taking orders from consumers. They said Taurus stood for innovative design, roominess, and performance—attributes they wanted to see enhanced in the updated model. They also asked for a bold design statement for 1996.

The result? The new Taurus is sleeker, less boxy, and more Porsche-like with its bug-eyed headlights. Inside, there's a new, refined integrated instrument control panel; a flip-and-fold-down, front bench-seat console; a body side stamped from a single sheet of metal; improvements in quality such as a reduction of squeaks, rattles, and wind noise; and a state-of-the-art, 24-valve, all-aluminum V-6 Duratec engine.

So how did the new Taurus fare in the marketplace? High expectations were tempered by early mixed reviews. The model received criticism for styling that was "too radical," for pricing that was excessive (the base sticker price was $17,995), and for lower-than-expected sales out of the gate. Yet the Taurus ended the year as the best-selling sedan in its class, and, at this writing, was ahead of the second-place Honda Accord for 1997 sales leadership. In the end, Team Taurus breathed a collective sigh of relief as its tremendous investment in consumer preference paid off once again.

BECOMING A "MARGARET MEAD" OF MARKETING

While the Team Taurus approach was effective for designing a new automobile, figuring out how to enhance your knowledge to improve selling other merchandise has challenged marketers to stretch even farther. Some of the modern methods of studying consumer behavior are as innovative as the work of Margaret Mead, the brilliant anthropologist who popularized the use of on-site field studies to understand life in the islands of Samoa. Mead lived among the natives, observing everyday solutions to human problems.

Today one can draw a parallel between the mind-to-market methods for understanding the "consumers in our midst" and those of Mead. For years, apparel retailers, as an example, spent a great deal of time talking to consumers and evaluating what they bought—both in their stores and in those of their competitors. As helpful as this was, a piece of the picture was missing—information about how customers were using their clothes at home.

Modern marketers for firms as diverse as Victoria's Secret and the National Football League Licensed Products division began turning to focus groups that concluded not with a thank-you, but with a request (accompanied by a gift certificate) to visit consumers' homes and analyze their wardrobes. Cooperating consumers take clothes out of their closets, place them on the bed, and explain how they put various items together—for work, for play, or for special occasions. By observing how consumers mix and match styles and colors, marketers gain insight into the types of designs and fabrics that work best for how their consumers use their clothing. Entrepreneurs, marketers, and company presidents alike might visit homes during real-estate open houses to gain access to consumers' homes. Some of the most innovative companies position cameras inside consumers' homes (with their consent) to observe how they live. Cameras may be installed in kitchens, closets, or other locations to observe firsthand how consumers handle, store, and organize products and solve problems. These tapes take the Team Taurus approach one step further by allowing people in marketing, engineering, and finance to watch how consumers solve problems for which no products have yet been designed, identify new product opportunities, and observe how consumers use the products in their homes (which is often different from how they were intended to be used). Such research can lead to product redesign or a new marketing angle for advertising.

KNOWLEDGE-BASED STRATEGIES

The bridge leading from consumers' minds to strategic marketing plans (and back again) is paved with stepping stones of knowledge gleaned from the latest in the fields of economics, sociology, demographics, psychology, and anthropology. Strategies that propel product information and solutions into the minds of consumers include developing and positioning strong brands, employee training, niche leadership, and unprecedented levels and forms of customer service.

Techniques that will ensure a company's ability to meet the consumer's wants include a commitment to a program of ongoing research. In its quest to become one of the strongest lingerie brands in the world, in 1996 Victoria's Secret implemented a continual research system to talk to and monitor its current and would-be customers. Rather than relying on one-time research projects to help guide its branding strategies, the company has made a commitment to a long-term consumer-monitoring system to pump an ongoing stream of knowledge through its corporate veins.

Victoria's Secret's continuous brand-tracking research program was designed to follow the progress of brand loyalty among lingerie buyers. By conducting 2,400 telephone interviews per year with women aged 18 to 45, the company hopes to learn the extent of consumers' commitment to the brand as well as to find out which marketing activities most enhance that commitment. During telephone surveys, consumers answer questions about the image of VS (as well as its competitors), product strengths and weaknesses, and store image. Inarguably, many mind-to-market leaders will implement similar types of continual knowledge systems to provide long-term guidance on how to adapt to consumer needs.

Implementing strategies based on logistics knowledge and the ability to solve customers' transportation needs has likewise helped to propel the earnings of AirNet Systems Inc., an Ohio-based air freight company, into the stratosphere. Gerald G. Mercer started the company in 1974 in Pontiac, Michigan, with $50. Now he is CEO of AirNet, with $76 million in revenue and 98 planes, including 28 Learjets and 70 light twins, which fly to 85 cities in 40 states. Its U.S. Check division is the nation's largest transporter of canceled checks and related materials, a market niche that has proven highly profitable. In fact, because AirNet dominates this niche, it competes directly and successfully with a rather impressive giant—the Federal Reserve Bank.

In 1989, AirNet developed a high-priority, small-package delivery service, called TIMEXPRESS, which appealed to firms that need parts and packages "an hour ago." Customers can tender a package to AirNet as late as 3:00 A.M. and still have guaranteed delivery by 9:00 A.M. the next business day to hundreds of U.S. locations, a unique service that commands a premium price. Positioned as a source of logistics know-how, its record for reliability and customer service surpasses even industry leader Federal Express, with down-to-the-minute flight plans. Just as Kinko's and Ford have addressed consumers' problems based on their knowledge of consumer markets, AirNet is solving problems for businesses based on its knowledge of the business-to-business market.

KNOWLEDGE AS THE STRATEGIC WEAPON

So far, the '90s have been the decade of reengineering and downsizing. From the perspective of the next century, however, these may seem like the "easy times." Inefficient organizations, be they retailers, wholesalers, or manufacturers, often in the past existed alongside more efficient firms. Traditional supply chains were saturated with waste, ineptitude, and duplication of effort, but there was enough profit in the total distribution channel to support these inefficiencies. Firms that did a passable job of producing good products at reasonably competitive prices survived—especially if they boasted a strong regional base. Megamerchants changed all that. When megamerchants such as The Limited, Wal-Mart, Kmart, Toys "R" Us, and others competed with the small independents, they won big and many small firms fell by the wayside.

The 21st century will usher in a whole new marketplace, one in which the megamerchants, having eaten most of the small fish, will be left with no choice but to devour each other. No firm—not even a Wal-Mart or a JCPenney—will be invulnerable to the competitive frenzy that will be generated by fire-sale prices of smaller or regional firms as they slash prices on the way to Chapter 11. Nor will any company be protected from the increasing selection and service offerings of the big-box, "category-killer" superstores.

In markets that can support three profitable stores of each commodity, generally five will be built. Two can achieve acceptable profits and one more may survive at the break-even point. Two will not make the cut when the team is assembled for the 21st century. The weapons needed to compete and succeed include having a wealth of knowledge about market trends, consumer behavior, technology, and logistics, and executing knowledge-driven changes in the marketplace.

While large, profitable firms like Victoria's Secret can afford to earmark sizable budgets for ongoing market research, firms of all sizes and profit levels can conduct their own commonsense work. Effective strategies include asking store managers and CEOs (and in fact all employees) to wear the hat of the consumer by walking through stores (competitors' stores as well) and getting to know customers, monitoring market trends through publications, and attending industry conferences. For all companies, staying abreast of the market means never allowing yourself to get too distant from the consumer's reality. The best approach is to integrate all of these mind-to-market tools into an overall approach of *continual knowledge immersion*. MicroCenter, Kinko's, Ford, and AirNet all exhibit the winning characteristics of firms that follow this approach to continual improvement.

Visionary companies will do all of these things and many more to gain information and build a solid and yet ever-expanding base of knowledge. Indeed, knowledge provides the fuel for winning demand chains. Without it, companies are doomed to a future of mediocrity, at best. With knowledge, firms can follow Gretsky's lead and skate not to where the puck is but to where the puck will be.

SIX

SHIFTING FUNCTIONS AMONG SUPPLY-CHAIN PLAYERS

"If there's a better way to do it, find it."
— THOMAS EDISON

THE BEST FIRM FOR THE JOB

In the past, individual supply-chain partners could be counted on to perform specific functions. Manufacturers were to design and produce merchandise, wholesalers (or intermediaries) to stock and ship it, and retailers to sell it to the public. But just as men and women in society have been evolving out of their stereotypical, gender-based roles, so too have demand-chain players, which have been increasingly assuming functions that extend beyond their traditional ken. Today, manufacturers may be in the business of marketing; wholesalers may design new products; and retailers may direct the logistical flow of the supply chain. And consumers—the end users and most important members of the demand chain—are also assuming some of the shifted responsibilities that were once fulfilled by retailers or others.

Shifting functions to the supply-chain members that are best equipped to fulfill them—what academics call "functional shiftability"—is a process that brings increased synchronization and efficiency to the entire chain. While shifting functions is possible, elimination of these functions is not. A number of essential economic activities, inherent to the creation of value, pervade the entire marketing process. Regardless of which partner performs which function, the chain must complete specific tasks. But as demand chains evolve in the future, the efficiencies in completing the tasks will change with them, resulting in cost-saving, win-win situations for all partners. Partners in winning supply chains will be expected to add value and efficiency to the chain or jeopardize their position in that chain.

The essential marketing activities, or functions of demand chains, are categorized into three types:

- *Transactional*—determining consumer needs, designing products to satisfy those needs, branding, pricing, stimulating demand, stocking and displaying products, and selling.

- *Logistical*—materials management, warehousing, transportation, distribution, and delivery.

- *Facilitating*—financing, taking risks by holding ownership, providing marketing research and consumer data.

Business strategists are beginning to plan for the fierce competitive battles that will blaze between supply chains in the future. With functions shifting rapidly within supply chains, strategists will be forced to shake up any chains that remain rigidly attached to the status quo. And they will turn to the emerging alternative supply chains capable of performing market functions more efficiently.

When functions within a supply chain shift to a more efficient operation, those entities generally increase revenues and become more profitable—a signal that sometimes passes unnoticed by Wall Street until detected by savvy investors. Managers, investors, and supply-chain members who understand the concept of functional shiftability will be able to identify organizations in the supply chain best positioned and equipped to add value to the process.

SHIFTING FUNCTIONS TO CONSUMERS

At the consumer level, the most obvious and easily understood form of supply-chain functional shiftability is from retailer to customer. For example, until the 1970s, most department stores delivered purchases to consumers' homes for "free," performing the most common logistical function of the demand chain—delivery. For major department stores, operating delivery trucks several times a week to surrounding areas for purchases as small as shaving cream was just a customary cost of doing business. And while delivery was "free" to consumers, the cost to the retailer was substantial. In the case of a product like shaving cream, it represented probably several times the price of the item.

Wise entrepreneurs and supply-channel members look for such opportunities to create alternative channels to perform functions more efficiently. Eventually, the supply chain learned that it was more efficient (in terms of time and dollars) for consumers to perform the delivery function themselves. And although home delivery would seem to be a dated function, in fact, in the 1990s, some retailers have revisited it by developing niches catering to time-pressed customers. Indeed, a number of upscale electronic grocery-shopping services have sprung up trying to assume shopping and delivery functions for customers. However, even high-dollar retailers have found the delivery function to be expensive, if not prohibitively expensive.

In exchange for increased cost savings, consumers are assuming responsibility for more and more services, including everything from gift-wrapping to product assembly. For instance, when they buy office furniture from Staples or Office Max, they can choose to assemble it at home or pay a fee to have store personnel assemble it. Some retailers provide specialized services for delivery, assembly, or maintenance for a charge.

Warehouse clubs such as Price/Costco and Sam's emerged partly because of their ability to shift functions to consumers in exchange for lower prices. In the case of Sam's Club, about 20 percent of its sales are to other businesses, especially small restaurants and offices. These businesses could buy from a food wholesaler or business distributor, which would extend credit, store the goods until they're needed, provide assistance in selecting the products, and provide "free" delivery.

Buying from Sam's eliminates none of these marketing functions. It simply shifts them to a more efficient level in the channel, in this case, to the customers themselves. Small-business customers buy because products are often cheaper and they like the ability to shop, browse, and buy at the last minute. The same holds true for consumers. By buying in case lots or blister multipacks, much of the storage, finance, and risk functions are shifted to consumers. The supply chain has been "reprogrammed" to allow functions to shift to more efficient levels.

Shifting some functions to customers works, shifting others doesn't. So, how do you know when consumers are most likely to be receptive to taking on some of the functions? Companies would be wise to realize that functional shifts work best when consumers are willing to perform them, when they receive price or time incentives in return, when they feel they can do a better job or are more qualified to perform them, or when they simply enjoy the task.

CREATACATEGORY—IF CONSUMERS ARE WILLING

Not all shifts to consumers are ones that they embrace, or even willingly accept. When American Greetings introduced CreataCard in 1992, allowing consumers to create their own personalized greeting cards at computer-driven kiosks, Hallmark quickly followed suit with Touch-Screen Greetings machines the following year. The concepts enabled people to customize their cards, including typeface, graphics, and text and refer to recipients' names, birthdays, anniversaries, or whatever.

The concept sounded like a surefire winner. Marketers berated themselves—why hadn't they tried it before? However, once the concept was rolled out, the companies discovered that the majority of greeting-card buyers—women 40 and older—preferred to buy off the rack. Time turned out to be one reason. Busy lifestyles dictate how much time is acceptable in creating a card. One CreataCard requires, on average, 8 to 10 minutes to complete. Another reason was that many buyers are still not comfortable with computer equipment.

When American Greetings launched the project, consumer expectations of computer speed were based on the capabilities of older, slower computers. As increasingly faster computers entered the market, consumers' expectations about speed and, therefore, creation time, rose dramatically. While young, computer-comfortable consumers were more likely to be drawn to CreataCard, they were also more likely to become disenchanted with its speed. The cost of upgrading the computer capability of the kiosks put a dimmer light on the economic opportunities of the program. Media reports indicate that in fiscal year 1996, American Greetings' earnings declined 23 percent to $115.5 million due to a $52.1 million charge against earnings to write off overvalued CreataCard assets. The company reduced the number of CreataCard machines in the marketplace from 10,000 in 1995 to around 7,500 in 1996. Similarly, Hallmark anticipates the number of its Touch-Screens to fall from 2,700 to 1,500.

But American Greetings hasn't raised the white flag yet. To try to revive the ailing product, the company has cut prices, added licensed graphic characters, increased computer speed, and repositioned the kiosks where young people congregate. Whether or not it will be able to resuscitate the product, the wisdom for any companies seeking to shift functions to consumers is to be sure in advance they *want* to perform a function or else the shift is liable to fail.

CUTTING THE COST OF THE FINAL RITE OF PASSAGE

Sometimes the savviest shifts to consumers involve functions that might be easily overlooked due to reasons of tradition. Smart entrepreneurs are constantly on the lookout for functions that could be shifted to consumers in order to create competitive market niches.

Lloyd Mandel did precisely this in the funeral-directing profession, which, contrary to popular belief, is a lively industry. After graduating from the Ohio State University, Mandel began his career at a Chicago funeral firm.

Based on the principles of functional shiftability that he'd mastered in college, Mandel established a new type of funeral firm, housed in the relatively inexpensive storefront of a small Chicago shopping center. He had observed that many Jewish patrons grieved at home—especially during shivah, a time of social sharing of grief with family and friends. Many of these people preferred to skip a formal service in the funeral home, choosing instead graveside or temple services.

By shifting some functions performed by funeral firms to the home and graveside instead of holding them at a costly, well-appointed chapel, Mandel dramatically reduced costs in his own firm, which he called Lloyd Mandel Levayah Funerals. As a result, he was able to pass sizable savings along to his customers. (While the national average cost of a funeral in 1996, including casket, embalming, director's fee, and other services but excluding a vault was $4,600, according to the National Funeral Directors' Association, Mandel's average that same year came in at about $3,000, *including* a state-mandated $500 cement vault.)

Mandel's company grew rapidly. Citing low prices and excellent service, Mandel liked to refer to his firm as "the Wal-Mart of funeral homes." Funeral firms in existence for generations average about 150 families served a year. Firms that perform more than 300 or 400 funerals per year are considered large by industry standards, and only a few firms in major cities do more than 500 funerals a year. When Mandel opened the firm in 1989, he hoped to do 50 cases. In fact, he sold 108 services the first year, 208 the second year, 365 the third year and, by 1996, had grown his business to performing over 600 per year. Mandel began to franchise his innovative approach to other cities and continued to do so even after he sold the company in 1995 to Service Corp. International.

Service Corp. International, known as SCI, owes much of its success to practicing a form of functional shiftability in its own firm, on a much broader scale than did Mandel. SCI started over three decades ago as a funeral and cemetery ownership group in Houston and evolved into a global organization listed on the New York Stock Exchange. Its accomplishments—consistent earnings growth and the rise in its stock value—are impressive. SCI has produced compounded earnings-per-share growth of 18 percent annually since 1989, earning it a rank of number 10 in the Standard & Poor's 500 for consistency, right behind number 9 Coca-Cola with 18.7 percent earnings-per-share growth. In 1996 alone, the stock more than doubled in value, and revenues were projected to exceed $2 billion from its funeral-service locations in the United States, Canada, Australia, Europe, and the Pacific Rim. Among other firms, SCI owns the Paris-based Pompes Funèbres Générales S.A., the largest funeral organization in Europe, operating in seven European countries as well as the Pacific Rim.

SCI achieves much of its success by performing functions more efficiently than traditional funeral firms by operating in geographic clusters. The cluster concept reduces overall costs by sharing centralized resources. The highly fragmented funeral industry consists of roughly 24,000 firms scattered among cities and rural areas in North America alone. Each firm generally owns its own chapel and preparation or embalming facility, which may sometimes cost millions of dollars to build; add to that the cost of buying and maintaining a limousine. (The cost of a new hearse is now approaching $75,000.) Each firm usually runs its own advertising program, operates its own computer and accounting system, and conducts its own training program. Since the average funeral firm serves only two or three families per week, individual operators face excess capacity and extremely high overhead costs. While the public may believe that funeral firms are highly profitable, in fact, their return on investment is generally fairly low.

These conditions provide an irresistible environment for an organization with an ability to streamline and shift functions in order to achieve greater efficiency and lower cost. The giant SCI demonstrates its ability successfully to shift functions to centralized preparation facilities, share livery among many firms, shift operations to underutilized facilities, combine cemetery and funeral operations, prepare and place advertising centrally, and develop state-of-the-art management and computer systems that can be shared by all firms. It can also recruit and train personnel on a regional or national basis. By shifting and centralizing these functions, SCI has been able to reduce operating costs by 15 to 20 percent. In Jacksonville, Florida, for example, SCI operates a centralized transportation, preparation, cremation, and administration facility that efficiently supports the city's 12 SCI-affiliated funeral firms.

One function that proves difficult to shift to SCI headquarters is the development of a local image for each funeral firm. The company wisely elected to retain the name and unique service capabilities of its local establishments. Because funeral-home patrons are not attracted to a "national" brand, the SCI name does not appear on its funeral homes or cemeteries. And knowing that the local operator is more attuned to the customs and preferences of its patrons, SCI leaves nonstrategic decisions about such matters as interior decor and public relations to them.

Not every function in a supply chain should be performed by the same firm. In 1986, SCI purchased a firm called AMEDCO, one of the larger suppliers of funeral merchandise, including caskets. In this case, SCI went head-to-head against one of the largest and most efficient funeral merchandise firms in the industry, Batesville Casket Company, a wholly owned subsidiary of Hillenbrand Industries, another NYSE firm with an impressive record of growth in profits and stock value.

What happens when a highly efficient retailer tries to compete with a highly efficient manufacturer? In this case, SCI retreated, abandoned its own attempt to perform manufacturing functions, and developed an alliance with Batesville's largest competitor, York Casket. Among other strengths, Batesville has an unparalleled logistics capability. For a product such as caskets, where both transportation and inventory costs are substantial, logistics functions are often performed more efficiently by a firm that can develop unique advantages and economies of scale. Perhaps SCI and Batesville will eventually do business with each other, recognizing that both benefit by aligning with firms superior in certain functions.

THE SHIFTING ROLES OF WHOLESALERS

Though the number of wholesalers is steadily declining and, in many industries today, the entity has been virtually eliminated (with the functions they perform having been shifted to other entities), nonetheless, over 60 percent of manufactured products are still marketed through wholesalers. To thrive and grow as a wholesaler, companies need to perform marketing functions better than other supply-chain members.

Applied Leadership

One such innovative wholesaler is the Cleveland-based Applied Industrial Technologies. One of America's largest distributors of replacement bearings, electrical and mechanical-drive system products, hydraulics, industrial-rubber products, pneumatics, and related products, the company did $1.2 billion in sales in 1996. A boundary-defying wholesaler, the company has assumed a leadership position in the demand chain by taking on tasks that don't ordinarily fall under a wholesaler's usual "job description." In a traditional supply chain, Applied might be called a distributor of industrial-component technologies to such departments as maintenance repair operation, or MRO, and original equipment manufacturing, or OEM. However, one of the paramount tenets of a mind-to-market leader is its ability to assume functions that it's capable of handling, while in the process upgrading the entire supply chain.

Applied certainly answers this description. And at a time when many parts distributors are either folding or consolidating out of business, this company is growing at a rate of 30 percent a year.

Selling "Up Time"

Formerly Bearings, Inc., Applied Industrial Technologies was founded in 1923 to sell bearings and other industrial components. Today, it does a whole lot more. By getting inside the minds of its customers and solving their problems for them, the firm's real product is "up time," an invaluable commodity to manufacturers, retailers, and others. Applied's trademark is offering technological support to accompany its high-quality products and strategically supporting its supply-channel partners with products and systems to keep them running cost-effectively, 24 hours a day, 7 days a week, 365 days a year. Its customers include everyone from the little neighborhood mechanic to such powerhouse companies as Procter & Gamble and The Limited for manufacturers such as Timkin, Emerson, and Goodyear. The benefactors of Applied's "up-time" efficiency are companies whose profitability would nose-dive if faced with recurring equipment breakdowns and unnecessary downtime. Applied keeps the factories and distribution centers of these firms running continuously by linking them with the products of manufacturers such as Timkin, Emerson Electric, and Goodyear.

Link Your Customers to Solutions

One trait common to firms that assume multiple functions on the supply chain is customer orientation. Like Manco, another wholesaler that stepped outside the confines of its intermediary status to become a mind-to-market leader, Applied has made creating "jubilant" customers, in the words of Applied CEO Jack Dannemiller, the company's mission. You might expect to hear such language from a Hollywood entertainment firm, but from a parts supplier? It sounds unusual—until you get to know Dannemiller and his team.

Representing over 2,500 industrial manufacturers with 900,000 specific line items, Applied has put emotion into industrial products. Customer Jubilation expresses Applied's mission of exceeding customer expectations through continuous improvement, and it reflects the company's commitment to customer service. Jubilant customers mean many things at Applied. Foremost among them is the fact that the company responds to customers' needs 24 hours a day. In addition, it sets up specialized partnership programs and strives for a 100 percent rate of on-time and error-free deliveries. Company strategies for the future include expanded services, better purchasing management, improved inventory management, and total support.

Applied links different organizations within the same and differing demand chains; it connects manufacturers and producers with customers. For its customers, Applied sources parts and gets them to the plant in the most time- and cost-efficient ways possible. The company lives by the credo that total quality—measured by the customer's, not its own, standards—is the only way to create customers who are totally satisfied with the products and services they receive.

How does Applied really do it?

The "how to" that works so well for the company is shown in Figure 6.1. The process outlined in this chart helped revitalize a company that had at one time grown stagnant in sales and profitability. While traditional firms in the supply chain are consolidating and liquidating, Applied's profits continue to grow. Revenues have more than doubled in the past eight years.

What essential elements of mind-to-market leadership are used at Applied?

The inputs are shown on the left side of Figure 6.1. They include people, capital investment, supplier alliances, locations and facilities, and information systems—all elements found in the planning models of most successful firms. The outputs of Applied's corporate system are featured on the right side of the chart. They include measures of growth for strategic business units (shareholder return and sales per associate), logistics (inventory turns and logistics costs as a percentage of sales), systems technology (transaction speed and knowledge transfer), and service indicators (customer recognition, documented cost savings, and quality index scores). Top-quality service receives much attention at Applied, with framed letters of acclaim from vendors and customers lining the walls at company headquarters and branch offices.

Open dialogue with customers and vendors creates an environment of continuous improvement, which without trust would be difficult to achieve. Applied monitors its performance on various "quality indicators" in regularly scheduled meetings with customers and vendors. Only through open communication, based on trust, can the company know how to improve its key inputs and achieve better outputs. The result? Cost savings and high quality for the customer, increased sales per associate for employees, and increased shareholder return for the investor.

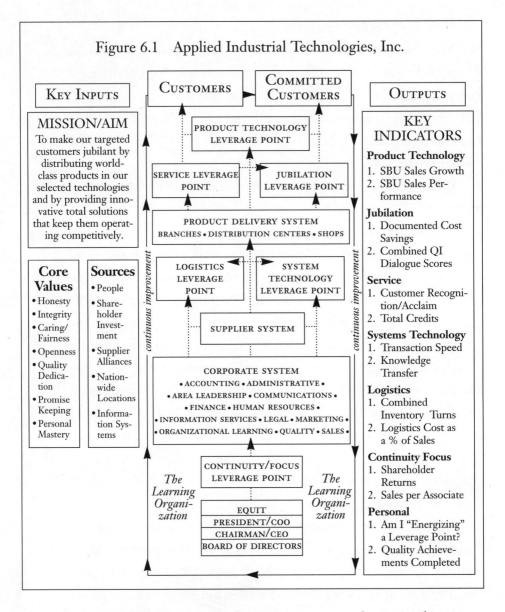

Figure 6.1   Applied Industrial Technologies, Inc.

Applied's system transformation process, shown in the center portion of the chart, intrigues most outsiders. The priorities of the company are illustrated clearly, with customers appearing at the top and the CEO and board of directors appearing at the bottom. A closer look reveals two types of customers common among most firms. Most firms will accept *normal customers* (shown on the left side of the chart), but for process partnerships to work well, a firm needs *committed customers*. Such customers are willing to invest in the technology and systems that create a demand chain instead of a supply chain. But this commitment is not just about technology and money. It is about communication—sharing ideas and information based on clearly stated values.

One way Applied works to stay on top of developments among its process partners is by installing employees in their facilities so that Applied will remain in the loop when decisions are made about technology, systems, and services. These employees, in turn, share their knowledge about how Applied can help its supply-chain partners achieve quality and cost improvements.

A CARDINAL AMONG WHOLESALERS

Another wholesaler that has deftly shifted functions and carved out a cozy niche in its demand chain is Cardinal Health Inc., a nearly $9 billion supply-chain leader that has taken the health-care industry by storm. The company started in 1971 as Cardinal Foods, a grocery wholesaler that served small retailers. Under the leadership of chairman and CEO Robert D. Walter, the Dublin, Ohio–based company grew its earnings to $160 million in 1996.

Cardinal Health performs many of the functions that were once performed by the retailers and manufacturers in its demand chain. For example, it provides sales and credit functions for the large pharmaceutical companies whose expertise lies more with the development of products than in their distribution. For drug retailers and hospitals, a wholesaler such as Cardinal stores, warehouses, and controls inventory more efficiently than the retailers and hospitals can. This is especially true for highly specialized pharmaceutical products, which carry a myriad of technical and regulatory concerns.

Cardinal achieved its success in true mind-to-market fashion by monitoring consumer purchasing data while at the same time maintaining superior product knowledge for both itself and other channel members. The company also develops the logistics systems required for shipping and inventory replenishment based on this information.

A large and efficient wholesaler and demand-chain leader like Cardinal can perform these functions more efficiently than either retailers or their manufacturer suppliers.

For instance, you might assume that as one of the largest retailers in the nation, Kmart could deal directly with manufacturers and operate its own wholesaling functions. Not so. In 1996, Kmart and Cardinal Health announced an agreement whereby Kmart would sell the inventory in all of its 1,670 in-store pharmacies to Cardinal, thus transferring the management of nearly all of the demand-chain functions to Cardinal.

While staffing stores and operating them is something that a retailer can perform more efficiently than a wholesaler, managing inventories is a function in which a wholesaler is likely to have greater expertise. In Kmart's case, the latter was deemed more important. To improve distribution efficiencies, Cardinal has taken over some logistical functions. For instance, as part of its repackaging function, Cardinal buys pharmaceuticals in bulk from manufacturers and then puts a specific amount of the drugs into packages, such as an individualized 30-day supply. At the same time, it manages the stores' inventories. Essentially, Cardinal transferred functions that in traditional channels might have been handled by manufacturers or retailers to the most efficient organization within the supply channel—itself.

COORDINATING THE SHIFTS

As competition increasingly moves to the supply-chain-versus-supply-chain level, managing and coordinating supply-chain players will be a crucial function the entities will have to assume. This demand-chain leader will be responsible for combining several intermediaries into a single system, thereby reducing the costs that result from a duplication of functions in the channel. It doesn't matter whether the leader is a retailer, wholesaler, manufacturer, or any other entity in the demand chain, the responsibilities are the same—analyze the functions that need to be performed by the system; ensure that each function is shifted to the most efficient firm in the system; establish and promote a strong, ongoing relationship among all channel members; and reduce conflict and foster cooperation among members of the supply chain. The goal is to develop professionally managed and centrally programmed networks, preengineered to achieve operating economies and maximum impact on the market.

THE ART OF CROSS-MARKETING

Henry Silverman, founder and CEO of HFS Inc., is a supply-chain maverick who can reach consumers where they work, play, or travel with his nearly $2 billion collection of brands. This demand-chain leader pioneered a network of franchises that includes nine hotel chains (ranging from Ramada Inn to Howard Johnson's), three major real-estate firms (including Century 21 and Coldwell Banker), and two rental car companies (Avis and Value Rent-A-Car). The Parsippany, New Jersey–based HFS focuses on performing certain functions best done by a central intermediary, such as making reservations for all of the hotels in the network. It leaves the hands-on specific functions, such as hiring personnel and operating facilities that meet local needs, to individual franchisees.

Silverman has mastered the art of cross-marketing to promote his entire network of brands. Century 21 agents receive discount cards for HFS hotels. Invoices at Ramada Inn promote Century 21 real estate services. Century 21 agents get a commission for signing up customers to stay at resorts for which HFS gets a fee. Silverman points out that HFS has 160,000 real estate agents, and every one of those people needs a car. He sees an opportunity there, whether they buy or lease. The cross-marketing possibilities are endless, and HFS assumes the role of promoter and advertiser for the entire network.

Because of Silverman's expertise in leading such diverse demand chains, he is able to spot firms that will fit in well within the demand chains he has created. And HFS profitability due to its dominance in the chain allows the company to snap up opportunities. The company's $1.7 billion acquisition of PHH in 1997, a mortgage, fleet-management, and executive-relocation company, fits well into the consolidated, home-owning demand chain Silverman envisions for the future.

BEYOND BUSINESS

In addition to revolutionizing corporate or entrepreneurial supply-chain members, shifting functions has the potential of reshaping governmental systems, including ones as complex as the U.S. health-care system and even American public education. Nearly everyone agrees that the cost of health care is one of our country's most pressing problems. Recent reports warn that, unless significant steps are taken, the Medicare system may be bankrupt by the year 2002.

Total health costs in the United States are approaching 15 percent of gross domestic product, compared to under 9 percent in Germany and less than 7 percent in Japan—a serious problem for

U.S. business to overcome in its race for global competitiveness. Even though Japan and Germany spend far less than the United States on health care, residents of those countries live just as long and have dramatically lower infant-mortality rates, as shown in Figure 6.2.

In a market economy, the delivery of health care doesn't differ appreciably from services such as accounting, banking, or legal help. Functional shiftability in health care may be just what the doctor ordered to cure the system. Dr. Mom (or perhaps Dr. Dad), who used to care for her sick family, may make a comeback in the next millennium.

The explosion of interest in natural health care and home remedies indicates that more and more people in the United States want to self-administer routine health care. Many routine tasks, such as performing home tests for pregnancy and HIV and self-administering allergy shots and flu and cold treatments, to name a few, can be done less expensively at home than at a doctor's office or hospital. This system is already being practiced in many countries worldwide. In Europe, for example, mothers and grandmothers teach their children about herbal medicines and work with physicians who prescribe natural remedies to treat common ailments such as

Figure 6.2

	GNP Per Capita (U.S. $)	Infant Mortality Rate*	Life Expectancy		
			Total	Male	Female
Japan	$31,450	4.3	79	76	83
Germany	$23,560	5.8	76	73	79
United States	$24,750	8.0	76	72	79

*Infant deaths per 1,000 live births

Source: *1995 World Population Data Sheet*, Population Reference Bureau, Inc.

colds, heart palpitations, headaches, and menstrual cramps. In South America, hospitals grow herbs in their gardens because medication is so expensive. Though natural remedies remain relatively uncommon among Americans, that's starting to change.

I often characterize the American medical system as a "sickness-care" rather than a "health-care" system. (While the former devotes most of its resources and focus to treating the sick, the latter would focus heavily on prevention along with treatment.) Many would agree that most health-care organizations are just now starting to focus on the consumer, leaving many opportunities for forward-thinking organizations in the health-care supply chain.

Essentially, health care is a cottage industry with hospitals and physicians acting as the "retailers" of health-care services. Competitive conditions change so rapidly, however, that increasing patronage is causing alternative supply channels to mushroom, and hospitals increasingly to be owned by large organizations capable of shifting many functions to more efficient levels.

A major success story among these alternative systems is the health maintenance organization, or HMO, that gained prominence in the 1980s. Does shifting health care to alternative supply channels such as HMOs really lower costs?

You bet. The more HMOs dominate an area, the lower the total health-care costs in that area. But the importance lies not just in how many people use HMOs but how strong they are in a market. Strong HMOs cause other health-care providers to lower their costs as well. According to the research firm Sanford C. Bernstein, the total health-care costs to employers per employee are $1,395 per year in California, $1,550 in the Midwest, and $1,900 in New York and the Northeast. The reason for the difference? The fact that HMOs represent a larger piece of the health-care pie in California than elsewhere in the United States.

Despite HMOs' reputation as being cost-cutters, most have yet to embrace a wellness-care approach. Except for the occasional program directed toward substance abuse, smoking cessation, and breast-cancer detection, most HMOs have yet to step outside the sickness-care provider mold. Perhaps the greatest gains could be achieved with a shift of important functions to Dr. Mom or Dr. Dad (or perhaps, Dr. Nanny). The problem is that, as yet, no real economic incentives exist for this to happen. Aggressive organizations, such as Oxford Health, the nation's second largest HMO, are already paying for some types of alternative health care.

The present system provides almost no incentive for consumers to be efficient in the use of health care. What would happen if the same principles that apply to health care were applied to food? Assume employers were to offer "food benefits" to employees, in which all employee food costs would be paid by the company, except for a $5 copayment fee per trip to the supermarket. Whether consumers spent $100 or $1,000 for groceries, employers or insurance companies would cover these "customary and reasonable" costs of living. Would consumers buy hamburger or prime rib on their shopping trips? What would happen to the amount of GDP spent on food, food prices, and distribution efficiencies?

That's what has happened to the health-care system. Consumers have shifted most of their health-care responsibility away from themselves to physicians and hospitals, while expecting someone else (namely their employers or the government) to pick up the tab. In order to be reimbursed, the existing system forces clients to see doctors for colds, headaches, and back pain—ailments that nurse practitioners or physicians' assistants would generally be qualified to handle. Health-care consumers have become accustomed to the fact that "someone else" pays. That someone else may be the government, the employer, an insurance company, or a hospital that cannot collect from indigent consumers. Over the last few decades, the responsibility for payment for health care has shifted mostly to third parties. This is doubtless one major contributor to the dramatic jump in health-care costs between the years 1960 and 1994 of a whopping *3,429 percent*.

Medical savings accounts, or MSAs, are a solution worth further examination by business leaders. With this program, consumers are paid an annual allowance equivalent to their normal health-care costs and are able to keep the amount not spent on health care in a tax-free savings account. At least 16 states have already passed laws encouraging MSAs, and some companies already provide them. Tax credits for out-of-pocket medical expenses, higher deductibles in employer-based programs, deductibility of medical insurance by self-employed persons, and other innovative approaches would encourage further functional shiftability within the existing health-care system.

STREAMLINING THE HALLS OF IVY AND THE AMERICAN SCHOOLYARDS

Publicly financed higher education is another big-ticket item that warrants scrutiny in order to achieve greater efficiency. Though most people rarely look at education from a business perspective, applying supply-chain thinking and shifting functions along the chain could offer some remediation. In 1996, the average tuition cost (excluding room and board) was $7,000 at public universities and $17,000 for private universities, and it's rising more than twice as fast as general inflation. Americans spend twice as much per student in grades K through 12 as do the Japanese, and for that investment we receive results that could be described as marginal at best. Education costs, like health-care costs, are dramatically higher as a proportion of GDP than in Germany, Japan, and most other industrialized countries and yet achieve results that place the United States in the lowest decile of student performance among industrialized countries.

Based upon my close observation of various public and private universities over three decades, I believe that the cost of higher education could be reduced by 30 to 40 percent. About 40 percent of university budgets are for instructional costs, an area where great efficiencies could be accomplished by distance learning, or tapping into computerized and interactive technologies that are now readily available and being implemented by innovative, entrepreneurial schools such as the University of Phoenix. The greatest economies could be achieved by transferring the cost of doing research—about 20 percent of university budgets—to specialized research centers and organizations or individuals trained to perform this function, thereby allowing teaching functions to be transferred to the most qualified. The present system expects every university to become a mini–research factory, resulting in duplicative effort that is often not relevant to anyone except the individual hoping to attain tenure in his or her institution. There is not much reason to change the system, however, when the only rewards and route to the lifetime security of tenure are attained through publications in refereed journals. As long as the professors who jumped through the existing hoops to obtain tenure are those who control the rules for tenure, don't expect much change. Functional shiftability would normally explain a natural movement of teaching, research, and administration (another 14 percent of university budgets) to more efficient organizations in the higher-education supply chain. The 30 to 40 percent gain in productivity will take much longer to happen, if it ever does, because of the tenure system, which protects the status quo. The loyalty of alumni to their alma mater represents another barrier to change. In the K through 12 educational system, teachers unions also provide resistance to the notion of shifting functions, possibly as much as they did in the steel, rubber, or automotive industries decades ago.

Could a new system be adopted for education that is as efficient as Wal-Mart is in retailing? It could, if consumers understand the problem and demand change. Innovation by mind-to-market leaders in education could also eliminate dying universities and colleges in the way that inefficient retailers have been felled by efficient demand chains. Unless consumers demand change, however, the alumni of inefficient institutions may support their survival through contributions and legislative pressure much more than they supported the inefficient retailers that were eliminated by consumers who chose more efficient stores.

Functional shiftability creates efficiency along the supply chain and value for the consumer. When consumers can perform functions more cheaply or efficiently than retailers, they generally do so, usually receiving lower prices, better products, or more convenience in return. For companies, the same holds true. The smart firms jump on opportunities for improved efficiency, not only in their internal operations but externally along their supply chains. Shifting supply-chain functions enabled SCI to introduce growth and innovation into the funeral business; it let Applied sell "up time" instead of just parts to its customers; and it pushed Cardinal to soar to a new level of wholesaling success. Functional shiftability can also impact Jane or Joe Q. Citizen's life by providing insights into solving some of the problems of the U.S. health-care and educational systems—creating entrepreneurial opportunities galore.

All of these real (and hypothetical) applications and efficiencies that can and do accompany shifting functions along the supply chain have one net effect—streamlining the supply chain, which in turn enables companies to speed their products to market.

seven

SPEED TO MARKET

"The two most important things we can do are manage inventory and lower expenses."

— DAVID GLASS, CEO, WAL-MART

LOGISTICS DEMYSTIFIED

Once companies have learned how to shift functions along the supply chain to determine which firms can best perform which jobs and identify how they can improve their performance, logistics is called upon to implement those ideas. Logistics involves the flow of materials and products through a business or demand chain, including procuring, maintaining, transporting, and delivering materials and products through every stage of production from the source of supply to the final point of consumption. Made possible by computer power, streamlining the flow and expediting the product is all the rage in the business world today. And with good reason: Logistics improves the quality of products and customer service while lowering the costs of operation.

The emerging importance of logistics systems amounts to what the *Washington Post* calls "an invisible revolution in the retail industry." Streamlined logistics can improve the efficiency not only of

149

retailers but every member of the supply chain, dramatically freeing substantial sums of capital for investment in research and development, better facilities, and improved service. According to the U.S. Department of Commerce, manufacturers have cut inventories by 9 percent since the 1980s, thus freeing up $82 billion in capital to return to customers and shareholders. In fact, so strongly has business embraced integrated logistics management as a means of revenue enhancement that during the last decade the National Council of Logistics Management, based in Oak Brook, Illinois—which barely existed two decades ago—has grown to a membership of 11,000.

At the company level, when firms streamline their logistics systems, vast savings are added directly to the bottom line. What's more, customers receive products more efficiently and in better condition. No doubt, top-notch logistics management has become a necessity for survival in the marketplace, the foundation of profitability in the 21st century. You can see this reality at firms such as Hewlett-Packard, which practices state-of-the-art logistics management. Although well known for its product quality and corporate culture, HP's logistic expertise was just as important in bringing its personal computers to market in months instead of years.

1,000 HOURS

One firm that's demonstrated its superiority in logistics management and established itself as an industry leader is the Columbus, Ohio–based The Limited Inc., the apparel leader with a large array of companies including Express, Lerner New York, Lane Bryant, Henri Bendel, Structures, Galyan's Sporting Goods Stores, Victoria's Secret, Bath & Body Works, Cacique, Penhaligon's, Gryphon, and Abercrombie & Fitch. The Limited's stated company goal is to bring a product from the mind of the customer to her body in 1,000 hours, or about six weeks' time. Accomplishing this ambitious goal as it does for many of its products gave the company huge time and cost savings over its competitors in the department-store and specialty-retail business, which traditionally took five months or longer to complete the same function. For The Limited, getting products to the stores months before its competitors allowed it to reorder only the most popular colors and styles based on the sales performance of the item while the competition was still stocking its first runs. On the retail level, this meant stores operated with fewer markdowns and stockouts and were more likely to have what the consumer wanted at the peak of the season. While the logistics gap between The Limited and its competitors has tightened, logistics efficiency continues to be a crucial competitive advantage for each of The Limited's divisions

Leslie Wexner founded The Limited in 1963 with one store, a $5,000 investment, and a commitment to what he calls "customer intimacy." Its flagship brand of apparel stores is The Limited, a leader in women's apparel since the 1970s that established its reputation as a fashion leader with trendy clothing, matched to the lifestyles and budgets of contemporary women. By 1996, that one store had grown to over 6,000 stores with sales of nearly $8 billion. How was this accomplished?

Analysts attribute this tremendous growth to the company's constant evolution of its network of organizations—based on changes in consumer demand, demographics, and psychographics—and, last but not least, refining its logistics systems. In fact, The Limited's famous logistics system has become the industrywide standard by which other retailers judge themselves. It's a system mind-to-market leaders would be wise to adopt in some form, and one that emerging companies in the 21st century should strive to emulate.

Here's how The Limited works its magic and speeds its products to market:

1: Prior to the season, buyers analyze data from the company's data warehouse and search the world for new fabrics and styles that might be popular with consumers in The Limited's various stores.

2: These fashion ideas and trends are immediately sent to The Limited's stable of top designers at corporate headquarters, who come up with the season's designs. Mast Industries, a manufacturing company owned by The Limited, Inc., is brought into the loop for its input on design development.

3: At "warp" speed, the designers dispatch these designs via satellite (or fax) to manufacturing facilities wherever producers can turn out quality goods while coordinating fabrics and other logistics with vendors. Most of these independent producers are specialists in "manufacturing to design." Since they've formed such close relationships with The Limited, they function with the speed and quality of a firm's own manufacturing plant while still retaining the efficiency and flexibility of independent suppliers.

4: These producers rapidly supply the company with bids, usually within three days; buyers at The Limited or Mast Industries select the right facility within hours, or even minutes, and award a contract.

5: Within three weeks of receiving the design, the manufacturer ships much of the merchandise on Boeing 747s to The Limited's distribution center in Columbus, Ohio. (Competitors traditionally shipped by water.)

6: The Limited's massive distribution center unpacks, reassembles, and ships the products with such blazing speed that most merchandise is in and out of the distribution center within 18 to 24 hours. Some of the merchandise is "cross-docked" at the rate of nearly 25,000 units an hour, meaning that the computers coordinate delivery so tightly that merchandise is unloaded from the airplane to the delivery trucks without ever entering a warehouse.

7: A merchandising team member at The Limited receives continuous consumer feedback about fashions, styles, and wants from the Information Technology, or IT, team. The IT team monitors high-volume stores every two hours to discover changes in consumer preferences for styles, color, and sizes and projects what stock needs to be replenished.

8: Visual displays for The Limited's stores are centrally planned, frequently changed, and dramatically executed so that what consumers see on the walls matches what's on the racks.

9: The firm's IT and logistics systems function with state-of-the art technologies, so that rapidly moving merchandise is replenished and items featured on wall art are usually in stock, meeting instantly the needs and desires of consumers.

10: The Limited's highly trained associates work to meet customers' expectations in friendliness and helpfulness. To this end, associates are often hired because they match the customer profile. To cap the sale, associates emphasize that "no sale is ever final."

While the goal at The Limited is to speed consumer ideas to market within 1,000 hours of their conceptualization, the actual average for the process is 760 hours—making the company a leader in the logistics field among firms of all sizes and from all industries. The Limited has become so efficient at the entire process that management is considering raising the bar and setting even more aggressive goals. Attaining such "real-time" operating objectives by a firm selling physical goods is equivalent to retrieving a customer's bank balance instantly at a financial institution or an airline retrieving reservation data on demand.

Even in the best of times, the apparel market is a tough competitive arena, and recently many retailing firms have been hit by the equivalent of a financial hurricane. In today's sink-or-swim environment, department stores such as Federated and Macy's have gone belly-up as did discount chains such as Caldor, Bradlees, and Jamesway. Yet, in 1995, the same year that many competitors wrote Chapter 11 in their corporate books, The Limited opened 504 stores. The Limited's superior logistics systems, its integrated approach to manufacturing, marketing, and retailing, and its continuous restructuring kept its balance sheet healthy and revenues rising in the hypercompetitive world of apparel retailing.

THE NEW IMPERATIVE

Logistics is the new imperative of mind-to-market leaders for two reasons: cost and service. In most firms, 20 to 40 percent of total product costs are controllable logistics costs, which when cut, go directly to a company's bottom line. Streamlining logistics can have a tremendous impact on the bottom line. By decreasing investment in fixed assets such as warehouses, materials, railcars, tractor-trailers, ships, and the like, as well as inventory, firms can hike profits—in most cases more easily than by increasing sales volume. These are some of the activities Wal-Mart's CEO David Glass probably had in mind in the quotation at the beginning of the chapter when he said, "The two most important things we can do are manage inventory and lower expenses."

For example, to increase profits in a typical firm by $20,000, that firm would have to sell an extra $1 million of product (assuming that net profits are at the standard in most industries of .02 percent of sales). If a logistics expert examines the materials handling or distribution systems in a firm and is able to cut out $20,000 of cost, 100 percent of that goes to the bottom line.

Enhanced customer service is the other goal of improved logistics. Logistics management controls how firms and supply chains perform in the marketplace, affecting the availability of items in stores and plants, and the time of movement and selection of items. And logistics management controls the speed of delivery—another prime factor that is critical to achieving customer satisfaction.

Logistics has traditionally found its greatest acceptance in industries primarily involved with physical goods, but today service industries are hiring consultants to help them develop plans for enhancing their logistics. As a rule, service companies tend to be less advanced in logistics management than companies distributing physical goods, thus providing even more opportunity for competitive advantage for service firms that can understand and employ logistics technologies.

At the Hinsdale, Illinois–based ServiceMaster, for example, which provides residential and commercial customers with a range of services from pest control to maid services, some of the highest logistics costs involve transporting personnel and equipment to and from work sites. A logistics expert might reroute service routes and bundle jobs geographically, thereby preventing waste of time and money. Each service business has different logistics issues, all of which need to be examined. If logistics improvements in service industries match the improvements experienced in "goods" industries over the past 10 years, approximately $20 billion of cost could be saved, according to a recent study conducted by the consulting firm Arthur D. Little.

For all categories of firms, logistics management is both a powerful cost reducer and an even more powerful revenue enhancer. Excellent transportation, warehousing, and inventory-control systems result in higher levels of customer service and satisfaction—

the ultimate creator of higher margins and greater customer loyalty. In addition to planning, operating, coordinating, and controlling the flow of materials and goods from supply to consumption, logistics managers obsess over the valuable information flowing from consumption back through the supply chain. Figure 7.1 shows how the flow of physical goods from supply chain to consumer parallels the flow of information from consumers and customers to the supply chain, as in the case of The Limited.

In demand chains, information about consumers drives the logistics system and determines how the chain ultimately gets the desired product to the right consumer. For example, information about how and where consumers want to buy their products determines the distribution and retail strategy. Questions might include: Are home deliveries more desired than in-store shopping? What quantities do consumers want to buy of a particular product? Answers to these questions impact the packaging and shipping decisions and functions.

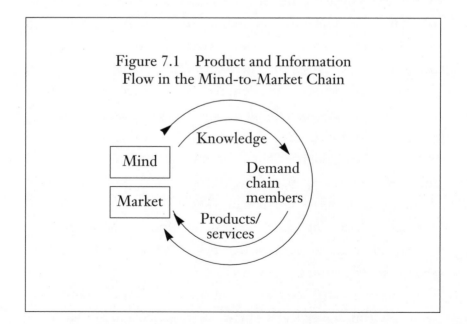

Figure 7.1   Product and Information Flow in the Mind-to-Market Chain

INTEGRATED LOGISTICS MANAGEMENT

Integrated logistics management provides a total approach to managing and controlling all material stock and flows through the distribution channel. It combines the activities of purchasing and materials management, usually associated with the finance and production departments of a firm, with the activities of warehousing, transportation, and inventory management, usually associated with distribution and marketing. Traditionally, the purchasing department reported to the finance or accounting department; raw-materials management reported to the production department; and finished goods inventory management (including warehousing and transportation) reported to the marketing department. Too often, however, each one hedges its bets, making sure it has more than enough raw materials or finished goods on hand to function safely—with little regard for minimizing total system costs.

In contemporary organizations, a company with integrated logistics management has to function as a unified entity, with the right hand not only knowing what the left hand is doing but acting upon that knowledge. Mind-to-market leaders, like Manco, weave this understanding into every nook and cranny of the company. "Our company's basic philosophy is that business is an organic process and system," says Manco's CEO Jack Kahl. "It's a holistic system. Business is like the human body. If the kidney isn't working, the heart's affected."

Mind-to-market leaders in logistics combine the departments (or functions) of purchasing, materials management, warehousing, transportation, and inventory management and distribution under a single, senior-level person, usually a vice president of logistics. The major building blocks in this new house of logistics are materials management and physical distribution management.

Logistics functions have always existed in firms. Regardless of size and whether or not they realize it, all companies, from multi-billion-dollar conglomerates to small neighborhood retailers, are members of supply chains and responsible for some logistics functions. Employing an integrated logistics system will help firms create internal value for their organizations and external value for their suppliers and customers.

Increasingly, logistics management requires partnerships with other supply-chain members, and these partnerships depend on an essential ingredient of demand chains—trust. When firms use "just-in-time management" (or JIT), "electronic data interface" (or EDI), and other logistics techniques, they depend on other firms to deliver reliably, at the *exact* time, and in the exact quantities and qualities promised. If you can't trust your vendor partner, the system breaks down in a hurry. Because of diminished inventories all along the supply chain, the results are more disastrous today if one link in the chain gives way than when traditional methods relying on large stockpiles of inventory as a safety net were in place. With contemporary logistics methods, a supply chain is only as strong as its weakest link. Every demand-chain member is faced with the critical question, Who do you trust?

While The Limited has chosen to own most of its distribution system, other retailers, particularly mass retailers offering both hard and soft goods, have not gone this route. They rely on their demand-chain partners to aid in their total logistics function. Often when these large retailers look for suppliers who will act as true demand-chain partners, they turn to Newell.

HOW TO "NEWELLIZE" A COMPANY

Newell might not be a household name, but business leaders, industry watchdogs, and smart investors know it well. The Freeport,

Illinois–based Newell Corp., which designs, manufactures, packages, and distributes glass, aluminum, and plastic products, exemplifies true mind-to-market leadership. Profits and growth run through the veins of the company, pumped by its megaheart of logistics know-how. The company, which sold $2.9 billion of products in 1996, set goals of achieving 20 percent or above in return on equity and earnings-per-share growth averaging 15 percent a year, which seem conservative once you examine the company's real power, knowledge, and performance abilities. Needless to say, it met those goals in 1996, in part because it sells to the big guys—Wal-Mart, Home Depot, and Staples/Office Depot to name a few. With a tenfold stock-price increase in the last 10 years, Newell has outperformed most of its larger, high-profile customers.

In the minds of retailers, Newell stands for service and superior logistics, unsurpassed in mass-market supply chains. Newell's 30 brands range over a wide variety of well-known household name brands, including specialty-glass product manufacturer Anchor Hocking, cooking-utensil makers Mirrow and WearEver, hair-product companies Goody and Ace, window-treatment manufacturers Levelor and Del Mar, and Sanford and Eberhard Faber, the makers of markers and writing instruments.

Most of these brands boast tremendous variations in size, color, and style, and most sell for reasonable if not modest prices. For buyers, department managers, and distribution specialists at retailers, these products are tedious to handle because of the huge variety consumers expect. The large number of SKUs make inventory, handling, and ordering costs so high that retailers might throw up their hands in despair. Many wouldn't make a profit on them if they had to manage all these items themselves. With its superior logistics systems, Newell is able to assume certain inventory-management functions and thus speed its products to store shelves.

PICKING OFF THE LOGISTICALLY WEAK

Newell has built its company by acquiring firms that produce quality products and brands but are riddled with one of a range of logistical problems. These might involve "unacceptable order cycle times" (time from order to delivery), "excessive transportation costs" (because of too many small orders), "sky-high inventory carrying costs" (because of too much inventory), "uncompetitively high inventory ordering costs" (because of lack of EDI), and other problems endemic to an excess number of SKUs and limited logistics technology.

These problems can be life-threatening for most firms trying to sell to mass retailers, but with Newell's "logistics CPR," the company is able to resuscitate such firms. Newell uses its expertise, technology, and systems to fix the problems—a process it calls "Newellization" of the acquired firms. A lot of other firms could learn from the mind-to-market leadership Newell displays with its logistics management.

Newell uses electronic data interface, or EDI, to receive and transmit purchase orders, invoices, and payments. EDI replaces paper-based processing with direct, computer-to-computer transmission of business transactions. This capability allows Newell to reduce errors, shipping lead time, clerical processing time, and mail transit time, thereby cutting days off the order/shipping cycle. At Newell, at least 95 percent of all orders are shipped within two to three days of the customers' orders, and 95 percent of all orders are complete. The company's goal is to reach 100 percent in both categories. In addition to being in close contact with the customer, Newell also links with many of its common carriers, which allows continuous monitoring of carrier performance and order progress.

When Newell supplies mass retailers such as Wal-Mart, Kmart, or Target, it communicates face-to-face at the highest levels of both organizations. These executives develop technologies and strategies to make the supply chain more efficient. "Newellizing" the firms that sell to retailers sculpts demand chains that provide top-notch service to retailers and top-quality value to consumers. The process involves EDI, which starts with consumer transactions at the cash registers of retailers and extends to every level of decision making (from warehouses to corporate headquarters) in each organization.

The beauty of EDI is that it enables retailers with multimillion-dollar inventories to reduce the "safety stock" normally stored in back rooms and warehouses. Traditionally, retailers used safety stock to compensate for their inability to forecast precise demand and account for the so-called normal mistakes in orders. Today, retailers experience such intensive cost pressure that they want to eliminate as much safety stock as possible, or push the responsibility (and costs) of safety stock back to the vendors. While some retailers are large enough to force these costs back on the vendors, the overall costs to the supply system remain; they simply shift to the weakest member of the chain. When retailers and vendors collaborate on forecasting demand, updated almost hourly by information from cash registers, and trust each other enough to let the vendor ship goods without a person authorizing each purchase order, total costs of the supply chain decline. This process of collaborative forecasting and cooperative replenishment occurs when firms are Newellized.

Some companies have meteoric, short-lived histories. They introduce a unique, popular product, grow rapidly, and then just as quickly sprint to the finish line, collapsing on the other side, as someone else invents the next "hot" product of the moment. At Newell, there are no huge, triple-digit jumps in sales and earnings, but there have been no dramatic shortfalls either. Stability and balance are the rules by which Newell is managed. It doesn't enter short races or sprint events. Newell's superior logistics systems and dominance of its supply chains qualify it as a long-distance runner in the marathon of profitability and growth.

THE THREE PILLARS OF PERFORMANCE

Just as well-trained, finely tuned athletes strive for peak performance in the arena, so do supply-chain leaders like Newell strive for top-caliber performance in the commercial marketplace. More and more manufacturers, retailers, and wholesalers alike are entering "logistics training camps" to revamp their methods for getting to the market quicker and more efficiently. Some of the components they focus on include execution, speed, timing, and productivity. These can be characterized as "the three pillars of performance"— all built on a foundation of trust. Logistics management provides many of the tools needed to achieve these objectives. Firms of all sizes can develop tools for survival in the new millennium by looking closely at each performance component.

Execution includes elements such as how well a company designs

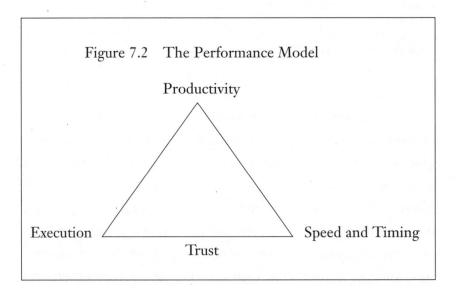

Figure 7.2   The Performance Model

Productivity

Execution

Speed and Timing

Trust

products and packaging, communicates with customers through advertising or the sales force, distributes its products, and satisfies its customers. Some athletes possess natural abilities and talents their competitors may lack. But unless these talented athletes work hard, train, commit to the mission, and execute well, they can lose to athletes with less natural talent, more drive, a better work ethic, and better execution skills. The same is true in the world of business and, specifically, as it pertains to demand chain management. A company's collective knowledge, structure, patents, history, or other assets may be greater or less than a competitor's, but the company with the greater passion, better values, and more enthusiasm often executes better than its competitors.

Prior to founding Wal-Mart, Sam Walton enjoyed modest retailing success mainly by executing the operations of Ben Franklin "dime" stores better than others. Sam Walton freely admitted that Wal-Mart was an idea borrowed from Kmart. His competitive advantage was execution. Rather than inventing some radical new idea, Wal-Mart concentrated on executing proven principles in the marketplace. Walton and his team executed all of the performance components so well, however, that Wal-Mart not only surpassed the success of Kmart, it now threatens the very existence of its formerly superior competitor. Regardless of how great a new idea or complete a strategic plan may be, it doesn't guarantee success if you don't execute with distinction.

Superior performance depends increasingly on how *fast* a company can react to changes in the marketplace and on the timing of those reactions. Too often, good ideas fail because of poor timing, as in bringing out a product that's ahead of its time or entering the market too late.

A company's response time stems from its culture, its core beliefs about responding to customers, and the motivation to serve the needs of customers. When Manco identifies a new product that can solve customer problems, it assembles technology, packaging, pricing, and channels of distribution at record speed. Recall the three-month turnaround it took for bringing a number of innovative products from customers' minds to the marketplace. By contrast, in some large, bureaucratic organizations, the approval process alone can take 14 weeks. Speed introduces the "wow-factor" into business-to-business customer service.

Timing goes hand-in-hand with speed. If IBM had developed its own software quickly for the PCs it manufactured, Microsoft might not exist today. Bill Gates created a structure and corporate culture to deliver DOS software—the right product at the right time, by purchasing another Seattle-based firm. The ability to introduce related new products, innovations, and technology at the right time often creates the fulfillment of opportunities that would be missed at other times.

PRODUCTIVITY AND TRUST

In addition to execution, speed, and timing, productivity measures are critical components of performance, especially as firms and industries mature. Productivity measures spotlight the variables that cause one firm to snatch victory from another. Competitors may also understand market opportunities and develop innovative products and channels, but in mature industries, the firm with greater productivity usually dominates and achieves the highest return on investment.

Whether it's sales per employee, sales per square foot (or meter), return on assets, asset turnover, stock turns, or gross margin return on investment, productivity measures help identify problems in companies or in supply chains. But knowing the numbers isn't enough. Managing the variables that enhance productivity always prove more important than knowing the numbers that measure it.

All of the performance pillars are undergirded by a strong foundation of trust—trust that permeates all levels of the demand chain. If entrepreneurs and senior managers do not trust frontline employees, a firm cannot act with speed and efficiency. If a supplier does not trust a customer, then the supplier hesitates to suggest productivity changes. If customers don't trust suppliers, they cannot readily shift functions such as inventory replenishment to their supply-chain partners. If employees do not trust management, they will not suggest changes that lead to better execution. Trust is the catalyst of progress in improved performance.

When you're shopping for a pair of jeans, you might not see all of these performance variables at work. But speed and timing, execution, productivity, and trust are all critical to the supply-chain programs of firms like VF Corporation, a major distributor of blue jeans based in Wyomissing, Pennsylvania.

A DEMAND CHAIN AS POWERFUL AS A BRAND

Most consumers go shopping for jeans to a nearby retail store in search of an exact type and size. According to industry studies, on about one out of three trips, these shoppers won't find what they want, often because retailers are out of stock. In such cases, consumers either take their business elsewhere and perhaps select a different brand or they simply go without.

VF Corporation solves these problems for retailers and consumers alike with a superior inventory management and logistics system. The company, which began in 1899 as a distributor of lingerie under the Vanity Fair name, sold over $5 billion of jeans in 1996, moving about one out of every three pairs sold in the United States.

VF's goal is to keep retailers' shelves stocked with the right sizes and styles and to keep consumers from leaving stores empty-handed.

Speed and timing, performance and execution. VF does it all, commanding its demand chain and offering logistics efficiencies to its retail customers. Wrangler, Riders, Rustler, and Lee—all brands owned by VF—might not be as well-known as the Levi's brand, but they're unparalleled in quality and price. Shop for your size in one of these brands, and there's a 90 percent chance you'll find it in stock. VF brands stand for availability and reliability among retailers and consumers alike. The company supplies everyone from giants such as Wal-Mart to individual stores called by such names as Tex's Western Wear in almost every city. VF's high rate of in-stock inventory compares to a 50 to 70 percent in-stock rate for many competitors.

How does the company do it? Its secret weapon is its Market Response System 2000, a state-of-the-art inventory replenishment system that serves 14 VF divisions as well as thousands of retail stores that are its customers. At Wal-Mart, for example, VF's computers track every pair of its jeans stored in racks throughout the stores. When a pair moves through one of Wal-Mart's cash registers, the UPC label is laser-scanned. VF's computerized logistics system dispatches information that will send a new pair within hours from its factories. At the same time, purchasing orders are consolidated daily for all the sales that are occurring and relayed by satellite to VF's vendors. These partners start materials and supplies on their way to keep the flow moving and consumers satisfied. Integrated logistics systems start with a sale; they create mind-to-market demand chains rather than manufacturer-to-market supply chains.

VF designed its logistics systems to accommodate small retailers as well as large, which is a departure from many manufacturers that focus strictly on large retailers. Tex's Western Wear, for instance, probably does not have its own powerful computers such as those at Wal-Mart, but thanks to VF's system, it's not out of the loop with logistics technology. When Tex sells a pair of Wranglers, it links to REDI (Replenishment plus EDI), a simple and inexpensive electronic inventory-replenishment tool. (To hook into this technology, the smaller retailer purchases an inexpensive handheld computer. VF experts come in and help install equipment and train personnel in its use. The customer may choose to place an automatic replenishment order, by which VF assumes the inventory function of the store, or it can elect to continue ordering manually.) Sales associates remove bar-coded tickets as merchandise sells and scan the garments, automatically sending the data to Wrangler via a toll-free number. Wrangler receives the POS data and creates an order for the items sold. Upon receiving the inventory data, VF creates an order to replenish the depleted inventory. In the speed-to-market process, the buying function is not eliminated but rather elevated to a more efficient level.

This smooth logistics system heaps benefits on every member of the supply chain, including consumers. VF obtains brand loyalty among consumers, and its systems reduce expenses for retailers dramatically compared to obtaining orders through field salespeople or by mail. In return, the retailers receive free freight on minimum quantities, reducing transportation costs for the store. The retailer benefits from fewer stockouts, a better product mix, and increased turns, all of which add up to greater sales and profits for every member of the supply chain. In 1996, the company achieved a compound annual growth rate of nearly 20 percent, and all indications are that the company is poised for continued future growth.

Everyone wins with this type of demand chain, which represents the future for small and large flourishing retailers. By turning most of the replenishment function over to a vendor who can supply various brands efficiently, small, independent stores can increase their efficiency and profitability, enabling them to compete better with larger retailers.

KEEP YOUR ASSETS MOVING—THE INVENTORY DILEMMA

Inventory is material at rest; freight is material in motion. A fundamental principle in logistics management urges channel partners to keep their assets moving—and at the minimum level needed to keep customers satisfied. Control the amounts of material at rest and control the speed and costs of material in motion, and you can affect total costs dramatically. But how do companies know how much inventory in the store is needed to stay ahead of consumer demand without weighing down the distribution channel?

The answer is based on how well the demand-chain players work together to know the consumer.

Logistics management controls several types of inventory, all of which increase costs when stockpiled and lower costs when managed well. Getting the right balance of inventory throughout the channel challenges the best of forecasters and logistics experts, who continuously study how much movement inventory, lot-size inventory, fluctuation stock, and anticipation inventory to keep on hand.

Logistics causes trade-offs. Traditionally, logistics management paid great attention to calculating the trade-off between ordering costs and inventory carrying costs. Before the computer age, ordering costs were significant because of the volumes of paperwork, involvement of sales personnel and time spent by managers figuring when and how much to buy. Today, logistics managers have added the needs of consumers—called stockout costs—into the equation. It's a delicate balance between the higher cost of holding extra inventory versus the ability to satisfy consumer demand for products.

Mind-to-market leaders turn to inventory control and management to solve the trade-off dilemma. For example, although extra inventory in the channel (housed either in warehouses or at the retail location) helps cushion the shock from unpredictable fluctuations in consumer demand, the costs for retailers to carry them directly affect their profitability. But customers are not happy when stores don't have their desired products in stock. The cost of stock-outs is lost sales.

Retailers such as Home Depot reduce the costs of holding fluctuation stock with techniques such as vertical space in stores. Instead of holding fluctuation stock in the back room, which costs as much per square foot as selling space, many retailers create their "back room" on top of the selling space, requiring no additional square footage.

While retailers lose the ability to compete if consumers can't depend on them to have of the items they want to buy, they also lose the ability to compete if inventory carrying costs drive prices above the competition's. Ultimately, that's why superior supply chains win. They balance costs and customer service better than their competitors.

ENHANCED CUSTOMER SERVICE: THE GOAL OF LOGISTICS

A focus on consumers and how to best serve them is the initial strategic element of mind-to-market logistics systems. This focus involves the art of identifying logistics-related customer needs and meeting those needs. Products do not have value until they are in the hands of consumers. Firms with superior logistics capabilities will get products into the hands of consumers quicker and in better condition than their competitors, thereby creating a differential advantage.

Companies can examine their logistics system by looking at customer service at different stages of the buying process. "Pretransaction elements" of customer service involve corporate policies to deliver service, structure the supply chain, and maintain flexibility of the system—all critical dimensions in mind-to-market leadership. The "transaction elements" are customer-service elements directly involved in performing the physical distribution activities, such as delivery. "Posttransaction elements" ensure that consumers receive the desired outcome from the product or service. Included are such items as warranties, parts and repair service, procedures for customer complaints, and product replacement. (For some products, such as oil, batteries, and even some computer peripherals such as Hewlett-Packard's LaserJet ink cartridges, which can be returned to the factory postage-paid, "reverse logistics" now falls under the logistics umbrella. Reverse logistics will be increasingly important as the emphasis on recycling and environmental protection expands.)

When high levels of customer service exist at all three stages, customer retention skyrockets. Information from computer databases and marketing research can help guide logistics strategies aimed at achieving high rates of customer retention. The best companies in the world will tell you that not all customers or all activities are equally profitable. When you know what items your best customers buy most frequently, you know which products you must always keep in stock, thereby creating customers for life.

Customer service, at all levels in the supply chain, will continue to be pushed to new heights. The pressure placed by successful retailers on other channel members will force channel members to exceed their current logistics goals. Mind-to-market leaders must work toward achieving the following aggressive logistics goals:

1. Eliminate excess inventory, including "safety stock."

2. Eliminate back rooms or stockrooms.

3. Achieve fill rates from suppliers of 100 percent accuracy.

4. Cross-dock a high proportion of shipments (transferred from truck to truck outside the warehouse) so that they're never warehoused.

5. Continuously monitor product movements with item-specific, electronically scanned technologies.

6. Incorporate automatic stock replenishment through artificial intelligence systems.

Many of these logistics concepts are complex. But the interdependence among the members of the supply chain is clear. In the future, firms will be only as successful as the supply chains in which they function. As logistics capabilities are streamlined and enhanced, companies will need to continue to evolve and fine-tune them. They can do this by examining micrologistics in house as well as in their demand chains. Increasingly, in the future, the competitive battles between supply chains will be won by chains that have members with efficiently run, consumer-driven logistics systems in place.

When reviewing the business landscape of today, several stellar firms—which have streamlined their logistics processes and demonstrated other mind-to-market leadership qualities—stand as examples of how to put all the pieces together to build profitable, cutting-edge enterprises. Now, we turn our attention to them.

eight

STRATEGIES OF WINNING RETAILERS

"Sensitivity to customer needs is our guiding principle. At our store, the attitude is contagious."

—F. Eugene "Gene" Rees Jr.,
owner of F. Rees Clothiers,
Mount Airy, North Carolina

Despite the recent advances in demand chains that put consumers on top and speed desired products to market, retailers and analysts alike have been befuddled by the seemingly slow retail sales growth of the 1990s, compared to the boom years of the 1980s. With shareholders desiring the return of double-digit annual growth rates, industry experts and academics have puzzled over how to get consumers buying again.

Some retailers have managed to achieve growth and turn handsome profits during these challenging years—in many cases by pursuing either unorthodox or old-fashioned strategies (or sometimes both). Their winning strategies can be pursued by any retailer. Foremost among them is customer orientation, which is a must for anyone in business. The reality today is that even traditionally strong retailers, like Canadian clothier Harry Rosen, have to get the fundamentals right and then push beyond them to achieve competitive superiority. Indeed, Rosen turned to computer-age methods to attract new customers and gain their loyalty, while shoring up lasting relationships with core customers.

FIT THE MIND, FIT THE BODY

Ask any Canadian who "Harry" is, and chances are they'll smile and answer Harry Rosen. "Harry" represents quality fashion clothing for men all over Canada. Harry Rosen, the man, is approachable, unpretentious, and popular with his customers. In addition to offering them a unique and upbeat shopping experience, the Toronto-based chain of men's clothing stores has always set high standards in the fashion industry, which competitors have tried to emulate for years.

A skilled tailor, Harry Rosen entered the world of retail when he opened a men's clothing store in 1954. In addition to managing the store, he continued custom-tailoring suits for many of his customers, a practice he's maintained throughout his career. By 1996, the chain had grown to 22 stores in Canada and one in Buffalo, New York.

Harry Rosen's strategy is simple. He provides a level of customer service that would make any great retailer, including the legendary Nordstrom, stand up and take notice. Formulated many years ago and followed today, Rosen's philosophy begins with members of the sales staff. Sales associates give customers individualized service and dispense advice, drawing upon their extensive knowledge of apparel, including fabrications, styling, and accessories. Unapologetic about the store's premium prices compared to mass merchants, they show their customers the quality of the garments, right down to how the seams are cut and what fabric is used in a lining. Well-versed in the latest looks, sales associates recommend when to wear new fashions and how to accessorize and care for the garments.

If a customer gains or loses weight, associates arrange for alterations on Harry Rosen clothes, free of charge. Crack a button or pop a seam? They'll be fixed at no cost. Associates also call on clients at home to evaluate their wardrobes and suggest what items need to be added to keep their wardrobes up to date. Understanding the value of time, salespeople will shop for clients and even deliver merchandise to offices or homes, free of charge.

One reason the system works so well is that associates are thoroughly trained before going out on the floor. New hires are given a week of formal training on "selling excellence" before they go into the stores to be mentored by a veteran for three weeks. This apprenticeship is followed by a week of product-knowledge training, in which they're versed in "clothesmanship," including how a good suit is made and altered to Harry Rosen standards. As a part of the store's extensive, ongoing "continuing-education" program, all employees get seasonal updates in which new fashions and fabrications are explained, along with information on changing consumer attitudes.

WHEN TRADITION MEETS TECHNOLOGY

Had someone told Rosen when he first started in the business that one day much of his success would be tied to technology, he would have doubtless pooh-poohed the notion. Today, however, he's not only a proponent of technology, but he's helped arrange one of the first and most effective marriages of retailing and database marketing—a feat recognized industrywide. In 1996, Harry Rosen shared first place in the Retail Innovation Technology Awards competition with Cyberplay, a retail store/computer learning center. The menswear retailer won the award for implementing a "proactive database-marketing program that empowers individual sales associates." IRIS (In-store Retail Information System) is the system that allows sales associates to see what individual customers are buying and when; it's also a system that progressive retailers will need to compete effectively in the next 5 to 10 years.

At the time of sale, associates gather as much information on their customers as possible, including name, address, language(s) spoken, item(s) purchased, brand, color, and size of each, and total transaction amount. When the client uses credit or debit cards, not all of the information needs to be keyed in by the associate. Client information can be pulled from the card and product information from the bar code. Associates are encouraged to add information about the customer—such as spouse's name, birthday, and preferences such as hobbies and pastimes.

The database keeps track of how much the customer has purchased this season, last season, and in his or her lifetime, allowing each customer to be categorized according to frequency of purchase and transaction amount. The name of the associate helping the client is also recorded so that that person can assist the customer again.

The system helps the retailer talk with customers and build long-lasting relationships. Amassing this vital information also helps the retailer form its demand chain, based on client needs. IRIS has helped associates bring first-time customers back into the store. Company president Bob Humphrey credits IRIS with increasing customer "recency"—that is, shortening the time between visits—by 58 percent over the past 12 months.

What's more, all of this information allows the store to target specific segments of clients. When, for instance, a new Boss suit arrives in the stores, associates can call up the clients who've previously purchased Boss suits and send them a promotional piece announcing the new arrival. The technology enables the store to invite higher spenders to a private showing, or if an excess inventory of size 50 long sport coats exists, associates can discount the merchandise and invite clients of that size in for a special sale, thus making room for new lines.

The system also promotes frequent and personalized communication with customers. All associates make follow-up phone calls to first-time clients 30 days after the sale to monitor customer satisfaction and obtain feedback. And associates regularly send notes to clients, call, and invite back customers who haven't visited the store in recent months.

SUPERSTARS ON MAIN STREET

But you don't have to carry the name Harry Rosen to hold a magnetic appeal for your customers. Indeed, some of America's finest retailers operate out of single shops in small towns, unheralded by the national media but superstars in their own realms. By knocking themselves out to serve the customer, by offering consistent, top-notch service and merchandise, by doing what they do year in and year out, and by being community players, such retail stalwarts are well equipped to withstand the onslaught of discounters and fly-by-nighters with bundles of promotional gimmicks.

A case in point is F. Rees, a fine men's clothing store in Mount Airy, North Carolina, a town of 7,200 in the foothills of the Blue Ridge Mountains in the northwest part of the state. With 20 employees, the company has become a local and regional institution, doing nearly $3 million worth of business in 1996.

Founded in a former Kroger store on the corner of Main Street and Moore Avenue by Floyd Eugene Rees in 1946, the company's three nearly contiguous stores—its flagship men's store, which now sells about *seven times* the national average per square foot of retail space, its fine ladies' shop, and its children's store—have 14,000 active charge accounts among them, serving customers from Maine to California, from France to Australia.

How can a small North Carolina retailer attract customers around the nation and globe?

The answer lies in phenomenal service, service at a level that parallels—and in some areas *exceeds*—what Harry Rosen offers. Going the extra mile for the customer coupled with good old southern hospitality has helped F. Rees build a tremendous, almost zealously loyal, customer base. For many out-of-towners, or residents who've moved away, no trip to Mount Airy would be complete without a visit to "the store." And when they do visit, after catching up on the news, they invariably go away with something in the trademark manila-and-blue bags. At F. Rees, a "small town" exists inside the store, whereby customers are treated as family members whom the staff tries to help out and in whom they take a keen personal interest.

The staff adopts customers' needs as their own—even when they're inconvenient or costly. If someone wants to stay and shop past closing time, the store remains open late. When a garment needs to be altered for a special occasion, tailors shift into overdrive, working after hours if necessary to complete the job. Once when a customer damaged his tuxedo for a wedding at the fashionable Greenbriar resort in West Virginia, F. Rees dispatched an employee on the three-hour, one-way drive to deliver a replacement in time for the party. No charge for the trip, just glad to help out. And, like Harry Rosen, F. Rees not only alters its own garments over a customer's lifetime, but it goes one step further: It helps out with garments customers have received as gifts from other stores, at no charge.

Possibly the store's most unusual attribute is extending credit at the unheard-of rate of zero interest, a feature that customers in college and professional school who are low on cash but long on promising futures find especially attractive. F. Rees courts such individuals, knowing them to be customers for life. As a result, the company carries upwards of $1 million in accounts receivable. And while it loses interest income, the strategy encourages people to buy more and buy better quality than they would otherwise do. Such long-term, unorthodox thinking has helped F. Rees build a formidable empire.

Though its customers are everywhere, a major component in the company's success is its strong grounding in the town of Mount Airy. The store provides what F. Eugene "Gene" Rees Jr., who bought the store over a 15-year period from his father, calls "a strong link in the chain that holds together our downtown." To that end, the company spends $25,000 annually on charity, compared to $7,000 for advertising.

Rees says that he and his 81-year-old father—who remains a strong volunteer presence in the store, continues to dress dapperly, and exudes warmth and a kind of Jack Bennyesque charm—have had some differences in approach over the years. But, says the younger Rees, "One principle that never changes is our commitment to the customer. Regardless of how we sell our product, that will never change. The fundamentals are what makes our operation click."

RETAILING: THE FIRST LINK IN THE DEMAND CHAIN

Perhaps the most significant change in retailing that's already occurring is the shift in its position in the supply chain. Rather than being the least important entity, it's now the *most* significant (excepting the customer, of course). Retailers like Harry Rosen and F. Rees understand this and are flourishing as a result. Indeed, those retailers who act on this knowledge stand themselves in good stead for becoming star performers in the 21st century. Just as Microsoft's

Browser or Netscape's Navigator is the gateway to the information superhighway, so are retailers increasingly the gateway to consumers. The retail store is the point at which most consumers interface with the supply chain, yielding information that can guide product, pricing, packaging, brand, and quality decisions.

As companies throughout the demand chain become more consumer-driven, they seek venues to gain greater insight into consumer minds. At Harry Rosen, the database system and the personalities of the associates make the retail location the first link of the firm's demand chain. As retailing looks for ways to reinvent itself, the most successful strategies are those like the following, which focus on profit growth through continual improvement and are driven by change in the consumer market:

- A shift from merchandising to marketing.

- Database marketing and data mining.

- Remarketing.

- Retail cost shrinkage.

- Globalization.

MERCHANDISING TO MARKETING: BEST PRACTICES

The best retailers of the future will heed market demands and evolve from merchants to marketers. The words "merchant" and "merchandising" carry great importance and specific meanings in retailing; traditionally, the career path to the top of major department stores required experience as a merchant. While for many retailers, merchandising meant marketing, only the merchandising function really mattered.

Merchandising emphasizes buying the right merchandise, pricing it correctly, displaying it properly, and taking markdowns at the right time. Proper merchandising would encompass such aspects as signage, point-of-purchase (or POP) materials, and visual merchandising. Although merchandising may involve some marketing, it focuses primarily on activities *inside* the store; while it remains important, it's no longer enough to attract customers to the store.

A marketing emphasis, on the other hand, focuses on decisions about competitive variables *outside* the store. Marketing-oriented retailers participate in activities such as defining and selecting market targets, selecting retail locations, designing the size and nature of the physical attributes of the store, designing and implementing information technology and logistics systems, and developing credit policies, programs to measure customer satisfaction, and other programs to lure customers into the store and keep them coming back. Many of these activities existed in the past, but the following marketing activities are emerging as "best practices" of retailers likely to succeed in the coming century of the consumer. Increasingly, these activities involve the entire demand chain.

Managing the Out-of-Store Environment

A marketing approach to retail focuses on managing, rather than merely adapting to, the out-of-store environment. Creating a "positioning strategy"—or a set of expectations—for the store before consumers ever set foot inside is a key tenet to establishing a marketing approach. Such strategies can be likened to putting a frame around the store that enhances the picture created by merchandising strategies within the store. Just as paintings sell better and for more money with a frame on them, so too will retailers make higher margins with the right frame around their merchandise (and indeed their entire operation).

Although advertising is the primary factor in creating this frame, merchants should also consider the following:

- Building and storefront appearance.

- Look, feel, and aroma extending outside the store.

- Store image.

- Safety of environment.

- Parking and store access.

- Adjacent stores and neighborhood.

- Reputation as community player or citizen.

Advertising for Positioning

Successful retailers advertise for positioning rather than merchandising. A marketing approach to advertising by retailers creates an image and set of expectations about the store, its merchandise, and its personnel. Rather than running attention-grabbing ads that scream out special sales prices, for example, Wal-Mart positions itself in all its ads with the line, "Every Day Low Prices." Likewise, Sears & Roebuck's major marketing campaign, "Softer Side of Sears," which helped to reposition the store, was a key component in the giant retailer's turnaround strategy. The total marketing approach taken by Sears involved fixing many problems and making changes in the stores *before* implementing the advertising campaign.

Had it invited consumers into its stores without first tackling its customer-service problems or changing its product mix, it could have alienated even more customers by giving them experiences that fell short of the expectations created by the ads. The quickest route to demise for struggling stores is great advertising because it brings people in the door; if they get there and are dissatisfied, you've lost a customer for life.

Retailers need a communication program that relies less on price advertising than an integrated marketing communications (or IMC) program, which includes everything from advertising and promotions to public relations and sponsorships. Such programs should be designed and implemented to provide reasons other than merchandise prices and sales to attract customers to the store. Mind-to-market leaders are more likely to use IMC programs to establish and reinforce a set of expectations that add value for consumers.

Marketing The Gap

By evolving from a merchandiser to a marketer, The Gap has enjoyed explosive success in our hypercompetitive retail environment. By late 1996, the company had grown to 868 Gap stores, 496 GapKids stores, 211 Banana Republic stores, 162 Old Navy stores, and 9 babyGap units. In 1996, The Gap brand ranked third in terms of sales of leading apparel brands behind only Levi's and Hanes. That year, the company sold $5.3 billion of merchandise and achieved a net earnings increase over 1995 of 28 percent to $452.9 million.

The company understands the importance of advertising as a part of its integrated marketing communications program. Its IMC program is based on a formula invoked by Gap CEO Mickey Drexler.

The mantra? Good style, good quality, good value.

The San Francisco–based company started out in 1969 as a

Levi's jeans store, before long adding other merchandise such as records and cassette tapes to the mix. Today, under the leadership of Drexler, The Gap reflects the disciplined marketing approach of a management team that understands the minds of its customers and how to please them. While merchandising is important at The Gap, other marketing functions are equally crucial. The firm is fastidious about the style and quality of its apparel and refrains from holding phony sales. The Gap's culture stresses cleanliness, and managers fuss over details—from keeping store floors immaculately clean to insisting upon rounded counter corners at GapKids stores to prevent bruising. The company has a high-tech distribution network that keeps over 1,770 stores constantly stocked with fresh merchandise. Buttressed by its acclaimed advertising, tots, teens, young adults, and graying baby boomers alike have embraced The Gap look.

The Gap's famous "Individuals of Style" advertising campaign gave the message that Gap fashions blend with everything from Armani sport coats to Grateful Dead headbands. Because of the strength of its brands in the market and in the minds of consumers, The Gap no longer has to rely on advertising as heavily as it previously did, but uses television advertising to maintain its awareness of the Gap brand and extend the image to new customers entering the market. In the last few years, Drexler has placed his emphasis on further honing The Gap name and positioning it as a global brand.

From Slashing Prices to Building Brands

Branding is perhaps the best marketing-based strategy that retailers can use to break the price-promotion madness that hit retailing in the late 1980s and early 1990s. After a few years of "buy-one-get-one-free" specials, retailers watched as this Band-Aid solution to hiking sales turned into a devastating blow to the bottom line of many retailers. Something was wrong: Either stores didn't have what consumers wanted, or, for some reason, people weren't shopping like they used to. A combination of changing demographics and changing expectations of retailers and products caused some of the best demand chains to turn to brands to entice and hold customers.

The almost constant use of discounts, ranging from 30 to 70 percent, has created an expectation among many consumers that normal—or nonreduced—pricing is unacceptable. But, among the most successful retailers, rarely do price promotions constitute a key component of sales strategy. Leading retailers reserve them for closeouts, seasonal promotions, or the occasional sales that contribute to the overall store image. Mind-to-market retailers create an urgency in which consumers say, "I love this product; I have to have it *now*."

Forward-thinking retailers will transform not just lines but their entire stores into *brands* in the minds of consumers. The goal?

Getting consumers to buy "the store" and not just the national or store brands it carries. When a store becomes a brand, it becomes "the only one that does what it does" in the minds of consumers. That's what happened to Harry Rosen in Canada. It's what's happened on a much smaller scale with F. Rees clothing store. Both retailers have reached a position that Hartmarx, Barney's, or any of the other leading men's clothiers in the United States would envy.

The Private-Label Solution

While many retailers continue to duke it out for consumers' mind space and patronage based on their selection of well-known national brands, increasingly the successful retailers such as The Gap, JCPenney, and Victoria's Secret are fighting the battle with their own store brand or brands.

No longer synonymous with low quality, private labeling is

increasingly popular not only among clothiers but retailers of all stripes. While supermarkets are looking to increase their label offerings to 15 to 20 percent of volume, drug chains have long sold their own health, beauty-care, and vitamin lines, yet they lag behind the supermarkets in terms of packaging. Lowe's, the home-center competitor to Home Depot, is developing a mechanics' tool line to rival the Sears Craftsman line in quality. Victoria's Secret extends its brand beyond its stores and catalog to a variety of its products including bras, lingerie, and fragrances, while JCPenney attracts customers with its Arizona and St. John's Bay brands.

Once consumers develop loyalty to a private label, they are more inclined to pay more to get what they want. The higher margins on private labels mean a substantial increase in profits. In the future, the best mind-to-market retailers will:

- Resist constant cutthroat and promotional pricing policies.

- Develop destination brands that will command full price and command loyalty.

- Develop the store as a brand.

Comp Customer Sales

More and more retailers are developing marketing programs that emphasize "relationship marketing" (in which long-term relationships between themselves and customers are built) and "mass customization" (in which marketing is targeted at the individual). These programs generate numbers and data about stores and sales. In the future, these programs will lead to the analysis of "comp-customer" sales, as Harry Rosen's computerized system would allow, rather than "comp-store" sales.

Traditional retailers measure sales progress in terms of comp-store sales, retail jargon for the increase (or decrease) in sales revenue for one year in comparable stores. (If, for instance, a chain has added new stores during that year, their sales would not be counted in the total.) Newspapers normally report comp-store sales of major retailers such as Wal-Mart, The Limited, Sears, Federated, and so forth monthly. But that's just part of the picture. When analyzing information systems, it's just as important to examine the data and information that these figures fail to reveal.

Comp-store sales figures are useful—to a point. But they don't reveal what's actually happening with the store's relationship to individual consumers. If a retailer reports a comp-store sales increase of 5 percent, what you don't know is which of the following scenarios caused the change: Did 5 percent more customers enter the store? Or were 5 percent more units sold to last year's customers? Or were the same units sold to the same customers at 5 percent higher prices? Another crucial question omitted by comp-store analysis is how many customers enter stores without purchasing products. Answers to these critical questions will help retailers understand which parts of the marketing program are effective and how the marketing and merchandise programs should be changed.

Frequency and Loyalty Programs

In the future, mind-to-market retailers will identify and measure frequent customers or "heavy users" in a market segment with relationship marketing programs. At The Limited, not only are a customer's age, birth date, and sizes noted in the computer database, but a note may read: "Ask about art classes." A number of retailers including The Limited have developed their own proprietary credit cards in large part to develop a more complete database and give sales associates greater access to the mind of consumers. Membership cards, frequent buyer (and flyer) programs, loyalty cards, and other methods of building databases track customers' repeat purchase behaviors.

Supermarkets such as Jewel and Food Lion offer customer-loyalty cards that track customers, permitting the store to give its best prices to its best customers. A major study sponsored by Coca-Cola found it to be more profitable for grocery stores to provide specials to frequent customers rather than the "cherry pickers" who come into the store and buy only sale items, which carry low and sometimes negative margins. Retailers with such programs may provide an end-of-aisle display with products at $1.59 for the masses but $1.29 for the store's best customers—those who have frequent-buyer cards. By knowing what's happening with comp-customer sales, retailers can develop marketing programs specifically directed to customers who'll increase their sales over the year before.

Frequency and relationship programs progress into networks of relationships. Today, frequency programs connect consumers with corporate alliances or relationship networks between airlines, hotels, rental-car companies, home-repair services, and eventually, most major retailers. Today the battle rages between airlines and hotels, American Express and Diners Club and Visa and MasterCard, to determine which network of companies will dominate relationships between retailers and their best customers. Consumers can earn points toward free products with every credit-card transaction. But the points are limited to the network partner designated on the credit card. Doubtless sometime in the future, consumers will be able to designate their own "portfolio of partners" to appear on a single credit card. Perhaps one smart Visa card will feature a telecommunications company, a gas company, retailers, an airline, and several hotels as partners. At the time of transaction, consumers would designate which frequency program to credit.

Scanning the Mind of the Consumer

When a high proportion of customers pay with either a check or credit card (as opposed to cash), retailers don't need to rely on customer loyalty cards to track most comp-customer sales. Scanner data provides that information. Indeed, mind-to-market retailers use scanner data to guide their marketing programs.

A decision that scanner data might help a retailer make is whether it should invest dollars in advertising versus reducing the cost of merchandise for specific sales. Manufacturers traditionally provided retailers with price reductions and advertising allowances to encourage them to lower prices, feature special displays, carry larger inventories, and design advertising to increase the manufacturer's sales. Should the retailer use such allowances for advertising and promotion or to cut prices?

Scanner-data studies of consumer behavior at a privately held Chicago supermarket chain over a two-year period revealed that price cuts caused consumers to stock up when the price was low— not increase total consumption. Advertising and promotions may contribute to increased total consumption instead of lower revenues, as lower prices do. Thus, based on this information, retailers probably will shift marketing dollars from price cuts to advertising and promotion in order to increase their profits.

DATA MINING

Victoria's Secret recently opened a new warehouse—different from any of its previous warehouses. It is a "data warehouse," filled with detailed information about what items are selling and why. Its goal is to aid allocation and merchandise managers in decision making rather than leaving a majority of the decisions to intuition. In 1995, the company initiated a test for the concept based on its bras, which Victoria's Secret calls "foundations." Because of the depth of the foundations merchandise (each style is stocked in 12 sizes and multiple colors in each size), it was sometimes hard to grasp what bras were selling in which styles and colors in which stores. Without the knowledge of which color, style, and sizes should be stocked in a particular store, Victoria's Secret missed sales opportunities in the products it didn't stock and was left with poor performers it needed to mark down in order to sell.

The test results were dramatic. Sales in the stores that were monitored and stocked according to the data from the program increased by 30 percent—without increasing inventory levels. Ultimately, this Victoria's Secret lesson in data mining shows firms can profit from the following information:

- Identifying which products are selling best in which geographic locations.

- Keeping in-stock positions on these items high without increasing inventory level.

- Increasing sales by stocking what customers want to buy.

- Decreasing stockouts and missed sales opportunities.

- Decreasing the number of markdowns taken due to stocking too many low-turn items.

What this means to both the average retailer and the large company is that you must be willing to spend adequate resources on gathering data about merchandise.

That's Entertainment

Do you remember a time when consumers went shopping with no specific product, purchase, brand, or style in mind? Those days are fast fleeting and that group of consumers is rapidly dwindling. While some still consider shopping to be a form of recreation, a growing number of higher-income earners now consider it a chore. As a result, today's shoppers not only want to come home with merchandise in hand, but they want to be amused and diverted while they're at it.

Some retailers have found ways to appeal to consumers who want their shopping trips to be an "experience" rather than a dull, transaction-based activity by putting the "fun" back into shopping with entertainment. Whether the product or the retailer is foremost in consumers' minds, how people decide to enter specific stores and what they do in those stores is of enormous consequence to the success of the retailer.

Different retailers attract customers in different ways. Some appeal to the senses. Successful grocery stores place a bakery near the front of the store, greeting people with the aroma of fresh-baked cookies and breads. The Body Shop and Bath & Body Works stores attract consumers with alluring scents and free samples.

The mastermind of entertainment retailing is none other than the Disney Co. People used to think of Disney as a producer of films, music, and theme parks, but today, the company is also a major retailer that applies its mastery of entertainment to its retail stores. Enter Disney World in Orlando and you land on Main Street. Dedicated solely to retailing, it is both the first street you see when you enter and the last one before you leave. Retail associates are trained that their primary product is "fun," that customers are the audience and employees are cast members following a script. Every mind-to-market leader hoping to thrive in the next century ought to study how Disney put good, clean fun and entertainment back into retailing. And they should take a look at the company's community-building experiments and projects, such as its work refurbishing Manhattan's Forty-second Street, the creation of the Disney Institute in Orlando, Florida, which offers Disney aficionados adult education, and the building of Celebration, Florida, in an attempt to create from the ground up a "small town," complete with front porches and town commons.

THE AGE OF RECONSUMPTION

Another sales strategy of successful marketers that will continue to expand in the future is remarketing, or the sale of secondhand or used products. Indeed, we have entered an age of "reconsumption." It's both environmentally correct and increasingly cool to buy previously owned goods; this trend is expected to explode in the future. So-called green, or green-leaning, consumers like the idea of using something again rather than cluttering landfills with perfectly good items. To this segment, purchasing a used item amounts to a double hit because they get to own something that's new to them along with the virtuous feeling that they're helping to save the environment (or at least not damaging it).

Remarketed products give consumers the opportunity to buy the same functional value of new products, but at much lower prices. Sports equipment (such as ski equipment, workout weights, and the like) is a prime example of the kind of merchandise consumers are inclined to buy used. Used sports equipment makes learning a sport cheaper; if one develops a passion for it, that consumer becomes part of an expanded market for new or improved products. By the same token, buying a used computer is often the first step toward buying a new one, just as used cars have been for decades. Today, in fact, most "new-car" dealers sell more used than new vehicles. While consumers pay less, dealers generally receive higher margins on used cars than new ones.

Consumers have always purchased remarketed goods through the informal sector of the economy at garage and estate sales, pawn shops, flea markets, and through classified advertising. Today, major retailers are getting into the act as well. In fact, the explosion of interest is so great that the remarketing of goods has become an attractive growth opportunity for large, publicly held companies, such as Republic Industries, the owner of AutoNation and CarMaxx, started by electronics retailer Circuit City. Remarketing is now big business.

Grow Biz, a fast-growing Minneapolis-based firm founded in 1987, operates Play It Again Sports, Once Upon a Child, Computer Renaissance, Music Go Round, and Disc Go Round. With sales of $500 million in 1996, Grow Biz proves that it's possible to turn a profit on used goods selling for low prices.

As a demonstration of both the growth and potential of the market, a recent edition of *The Wall Street Journal* published an article reporting that Herman's Sporting Goods (which sells new products) was closing 200 stores while remarketer Play It Again Sports was opening 200 stores.

With over 650 stores, Play It Again Sports meshes with the minds and lifestyles of its consumers, who CEO Ron Olson explains are "moms whose kids want to rollerblade one season, play hockey the next and then move on to golf." Grow Biz started with the conventional consignment-shop concept, and grew the business by applying contemporary marketing and merchandising practices. Today, with 1,087 stores up and running and over 300 franchises ready to open in 1998, Grow Biz is one of the fastest-growing chains of remarketers in the world.

Remarketing makes so much sense these days that even Circuit

City recently started a new venture called CarMaxx. It was the first to attack the $378 billion used-vehicle market with a superstore approach. But the second entrant into the used-car superstore field, AutoNation, is now leading this market and blazing a new path to consumers' minds.

Wayne Huizenga, businessman extraordinaire who has made fortunes with Waste Management and Blockbuster videos, has burst onto the used-car scene with Republic Industries' AutoNation. In typical Huizenga fashion, the Fort Lauderdale, Florida–based AutoNation is gobbling up dealerships and other auto-related entities with supersonic speed and steadiness. Huizenga is revolutionizing the auto industry the way SCI did the funeral business.

High on AutoNation's list of acquisitions was ADT, an electronic security and car-auction company. The plan is to use ADT's 29 reconditioning centers to refurbish secondhand cars, which it will sell in its 80 used-car superstores scheduled to open over the next five years. Each location is estimated to be 20 to 25 acres in size, offering around 1,000 cars—none of which will be more than five years old. As with CarMaxx, the prices will be set; no haggling allowed.

Huizenga's most recent acquisitions are National Car Rental and Alamo, which provide a strong clue as to how the company plans to consolidate and take command of the auto-demand chain. The plan would be to buy new cars, rent them through National and Alamo, pull them after a specific number of miless, refurbish them if needed, and sell them through AutoNation locations. The next stop on the auto supply chain is after-market parts and auto service, both of which are the focus of Republic's ValuStop chain. Remarketing is remaking the auto industry at all levels.

ATTACKING INVENTORY "SHRINK"

One perennial problem that retailers around the globe must deal with is shoplifting. They've been battling it for years, often hoping an increase in sales will compensate for their losses, or inventory "shrink." According to the University of Florida's Security Research Project conducted in 1996 and sponsored by Sensormatic Electronics Corp., American retailers alone lose in the neighborhood of $10 billion annually to theft. When combined with employee theft, vendor fraud, and administrative error, that number reaches a staggering $27 billion—or 1.9 percent of annual sales. The study showed 35.8 percent of shrink arises from shoplifting, while employee theft accounts for 38.4 percent. This would indicate that it's just as vital to monitor inventory in the back of the store as it is in the front.

Employee theft and shoplifting cause not only a loss in revenue but also skew all-important data along the demand chain. Even the most sophisticated retailers that monitor inventory levels with bar codes and scanners at the checkout counter are foiled in inventory tracking when stuff leaves illegally.

When the cash register does not record the sale, the computer indicates that the merchandise is on the shelf or in the back room, when in fact it's not. This leads to unexpected stockouts, missed sales opportunities, increased costs associated with reordering and purchasing, and unhappy customers. It also affects all members of the supply chain by giving false data on how much to produce and when and where to ship.

When shelves that house the most popular items are empty, consumers may migrate to competitors' stores. Even the stores that could afford to absorb the costs of this shrink need protection if they are to provide what consumers want.

CheckPoint Systems and Sensormatic are the two largest companies in the retail-security market—each manufacturing and marketing security devices to protect retailers' products and profits. This protection also increases the accuracy of what computers indicate and consumers expect to be on the shelf. You're probably familiar with the large security tags attached to articles of clothing in many stores today, but may not be as familiar with some of the latest technology being developed to help retailers cut costs out of their systems.

Shoplifters' CheckPoint Charlie

CheckPoint Systems, based in Thorofare, New Jersey, supplies many forms of retail security systems including radio frequency–based (RF) electronic article surveillance (EAS), Impulse source tagging, reusable security packaging, reusable fluid tags, closed-circuit television (CCTV), and burglar and fire-alarm monitoring systems. This technology enables retailers worldwide to surprise shoppers who leave with a stolen item with an embarrassing beep-beep of the EAS antenna at the store's entrance.

Historically, retailers have addressed shoplifting by placing high-ticket items in glass display cases or behind the counter—away from a would-be thief's hot hands. But when items such as jewelry, film, cameras, and consumer electronics are locked away in counters, sales are reduced as much as 30 percent or more compared to open merchandise displays.

However, by using state-of-the-art technology, this problem can be solved. Several generations evolved from the clothespinlike tags affixed to merchandise, Impulse source tagging embeds paper-thin labels into products or packaging during manufacture. Impulse source tagging places the EAS protective device on products at the source, at the manufacturer of the product or the package, thus eliminating for the retailer much of the labor costs of applying tags.

These source-tagged products allow retailers to monitor employee theft as well as shoplifting. CheckPoint currently partners with 450 consumer-product manufacturers to source-tag close to 500 million products with RF labels. Product categories include health- and beauty-care items, personal-care products, consumer electronics, and computer software. To prepare for source tagging, retailers around the world are installing CheckPoint systems throughout a number of chains, including GB (the largest supermarket chain in Belgium and Poland), Benavides (Mexico's largest drugstore chain), and Carrefour (Europe's leading retailer). In the United States, CheckPoint's systems protect stores ranging from single-store independents to megachains such as Target, Best Buy, and Barnes & Noble.

Drugstore retailers have been out front in installing Impulse source tagging. According to a spokesperson at Walgreen, since implementing EAS protection, gross and net sales are up, as are margins. What's more, the company no longer has voids on the shelves created by shoplifting losses.

And this is just the beginning. The greatest impact of RF-EAS is yet to come. In the new millennium, the next step is "intelligent tagging," or RF-EAS/ID, which combines an intelligent chip with CheckPoint's RF circuit. The combination tag will have the capability of storing, processing, and communicating product information, as well as providing theft protection.

The intelligent tag, which is attached to products at their source, not only tells the antennae (possibly satellite-based) that a product is passing by, it tells exactly which product is passing by—and potentially a whole lot more. A tiny computer chip, smaller than the size of a postage stamp and costing pennies to produce, could have the capacity to tell the logistics system when the product was going astray at any point: the warehouse, the trucking firm, the back room with an employee leaving work, or at the front entrance of the store with a shoplifter.

The intelligent chip has one more fascinating application.

Imagine filling your shopping cart with a variety of products, passing by the register, and receiving an itemized receipt without having to unload and reload your purchases. As the cart passes by the newfangled "cash register," each product in the shopping cart is scanned instantly, generating an itemized receipt.

The one significant difference from today's receipt?

No human is standing by the cash register.

Intelligent rf (rfID) has the potential to start automatic replenishment at different points than at the cash register. When goods move from warehouse to the back room of a store, the process is monitored. When the goods move from back room to the shelf, however, the forecasting model of the logistics system kicks in and predicts in how many days (or hours) that product will pass through the cash register and be in need of replenishment. Vendors get a head start on replenishing inventory and managing transportation functions. This continuous monitoring allows the supply chain to become increasingly efficient at balancing heterogeneity of demand and homogeneity of supply. The consumer encounters fewer stockouts and obtains lower prices from the supply chains that are continuously monitored to provide better value for them.

RETAIL GLOBALIZATION

With slowing population growth, depressed GDP growth, and a hypercompetitive retail environment, it's no surprise that retailers looking for growth are scanning the globe. Predicting which American retailers will be successful in the next century requires understanding retail globalization. Firms such as Coca-Cola and McDonald's now achieve most of their growth outside of the United States. Coca-Cola reportedly makes more profit in Japan than in the United States.

Global retailers are on the move—going wherever their products fit the minds of consumers. This international approach has worked well for The Body Shop (U.K.), Benetton (Italy), Eskada (Germany), and Marks & Spencer (U.K.). Likewise, McDonald's has circled the world, opening one of its largest restaurants in Moscow. Toys "R" Us does well in the United States but even better in countries such as Germany and Japan, where more money is spent on children than elsewhere.

Global Thinking

More and more mind-to-market firms are adopting hiring policies that dictate that no one should be promoted to a position of major responsibility unless he or she is capable of thinking globally. Global thinking is the ability to understand markets beyond one's country of origin. Global thinking includes the ability to:

- Understand demand worldwide.

- Source materials and services around the world.

- Understand management and marketing processes across national boundaries.

Many retailers and manufacturers have been sourcing globally for decades. But retailers preparing for the next century must also recognize the need for global selling and, with it, global management skills.

To understand the future of retailing, consider how quickly JCPenney is evolving into a globalized retailer. Given the company's traditional conservatism, management faced some internal opposition to global expansion. But a number of indicators put the handwriting on the wall that management couldn't help but read.

One company study showed that the 22 JCPenney stores located near the Mexican border in the United States recorded as much as 60 percent of sales to Mexicans traveling north to shop. Faced with limited domestic growth opportunities, the company has taken the foreign gamble to help fuel future growth.

JCPenney management traveled the world to understand consumers and their cultures in areas where they planned to expand. They found that in Chile, men consider short pants suitable only for children and that Abu Dhabi women, despite wearing full-length robes outdoors, like to wear high fashion party dresses under their robes. To extend a permanent line into the minds of foreign consumers, the company brought nationals from those countries aboard as managers and brought them to JCPenney headquarters in Texas to study merchandising methods. It also tailored the store design and merchandise mix to suit the customs of each country.

In "understored" countries where real estate is affordable and allowed, JCPenney opens and operates stores itself. Where high-priced real estate and local regulations make it too tough to own stores, JCPenney licenses local retailers to sell its branded apparel. In still-tougher markets like Singapore and Japan, where high property costs and regulations make it all but impossible to build large stores, JCPenney licenses other retailers to operate in-store shops selling specific branded lines. The Danchi flagship store in Hiroshima, Japan, for example, sells JCPenney private-label Home Products.

We Are the World

Intermarket segmentation refers to segmenting markets on demographic, psychographic, or other variables that transcend national boundaries. Such segmentation is based on the similarities among consumers regardless of where they live. Hanes's recent television ads showing its T-shirts being worn by people of all colors, races, and backgrounds living in countries around the globe make the point that the people of the world aren't black, white, Spanish, or Korean; they're small, medium, or large.

While North American markets are segmented based on demographic or psychographic variables rather than state or provincial boundaries, marketers often fail to use these same distinctions when seeking out markets beyond North America. Instead, they mistakenly revert to strategies that are analogous to implementing different marketing programs for each state of the union or Canadian province. Indeed, behavioral or demographic variables are much more important in an international intermarket segmentation strategy.

A prime intermarket segment is teenagers. Regardless of where they live, they tend to seek new identities different from their elders and share common characteristics, such as elevating celebrities to icon status. Companies such as Levi Strauss and Benetton appeal to this segment with similar products, advertising, and marketing programs around the world using the same music, slogans, and personalities.

Another intermarket segment is affluents who have more similarities than differences across national boundaries. This reality makes possible the global marketing strategies of Porsche, Mercedes, Gucci, Eskada, Boss, Chanel, and Rolex, to name a few. Saks, for example, is now opening one of its upscale department stores in Riyadh, Saudi Arabia. Other intermarket segments that exist in many countries include the "green" consumers, feminists, and others such as the do-it-yourself (or DIY) customers.

"You Can Build a House"

Wickes beautifully illustrates the concept of intermarket segmentation. A Wickes store is a Wickes store is a Wickes store; it doesn't matter where you put it. "You Can Build a House at Wickes." That slogan tells what Wickes plc, a British-based home-improvement retailer with 156 stores in five countries, sells. The original version of Wickes failed in the United States, but the Europeans created a unique do-it-yourself concept that successfully competes with Home Depot formats and has achieved strong international growth in the U.K., Belgium, the Netherlands, France, and South Africa.

Wickes developed the concept of "Glo-cal" retailing, shown in Exhibit 8.1. Wickes knows that a customer does not care if the retailer is a global firm. What *does* matter to him or her is what the store looks like. Global operations provide the scale and concept as well as the technology and planning to achieve superior supply-chain management. But the test of this approach occurs at the local level. Wickes calls it "Glo-cal"; I call it intermarket segmentation.

Wickes illustrates the advantage of starting with the mind of the consumer and implementing concepts from the knowledge and

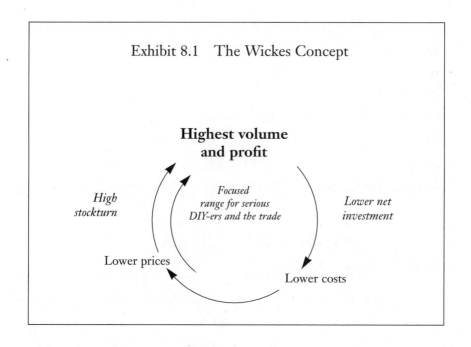

Exhibit 8.1   The Wickes Concept

organization triads. Wickes focuses on 130 of the most frequent home-improvement tasks and the consumption patterns of the DIY segment. It creates a total logistics system. The communication programs build a set of expectations among consumers that "you can build a home at Wickes." Its highly disciplined approach to retailing restrains Wickes from offering all products for everyone. It does not offer shower curtains, for example, because it realizes it cannot be the market leader in that category. As a consequence of its discipline, the typical Wickes store contains 3,800 SKUs compared to the 50,000 SKUs found at competitors' stores. As a manufacturer, you'd better know how to help Wickes sell what you manufacture if you want to be stocked on its shelves. This might be through product innovations or with extensive information about your products and how to use them.

Wickes, the store, has worked to position itself as a brand. Most of the products in the store come in only one brand—Wickes. Marketing and merchandising at Wickes focuses on creating a strong, quality image for the Wickes brand. Its brand is recognized internationally for quality and value. Wickes offers a highly efficient logistics system, creates high-volume stores, high-velocity merchandise turnover, and low net investment. This means lower costs, which are passed along to the consumer. Ultimately, high volume and high stock turns lead to high profits, as shown in Exhibit 8.2. You can see how multichannel retailers function in global markets with intermarket segmentation strategies by examining Wickes.

MIND-TO-MARKET LEADERS AND THEIR STRATEGIES

The retailers of tomorrow will be challenged to do a number of things well—from meeting the needs of consumers to offering

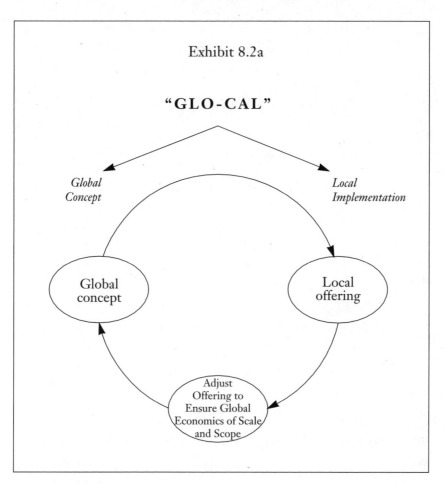

Exhibit 8.2a

"GLO-CAL"

unique personal service and merchandise, all the while instituting systemwide cost-cutting, targeted-spending, and micromanaged data-mining programs. You'll have to operate in a fiercely competitive context, one riddled with uncertainty. In part because many venues are available to reach consumers, in part because our overstored environment heaps greater pressure on all retail players, store choice for consumers has become a more complicated decision than ever before.

In this hypercompetitive retail context, everyone—from major retailers to individual operators—will need to take a long, hard look

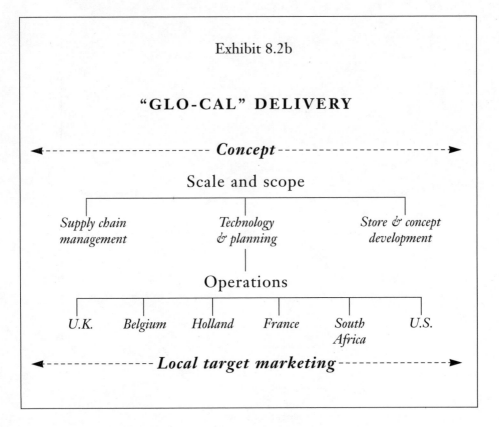

Exhibit 8.2b

"GLO-CAL" DELIVERY

◄-------------------- *Concept* -----------------------►

Scale and scope

Supply chain   Technology   Store & concept
management   & planning   development

Operations

U.K.   Belgium   Holland   France   South   U.S.
                                            Africa

◄--------------- *Local target marketing* ---------------►

at the strategies of winning retailers. You'll need to adopt or modify
these formulas for success and make them your own, all the while
evolving your own brand of mind-to-market leadership. Once
you've done this, the winning retailers of tomorrow will need to
turn their attention to the future and focus on the retailing possibilities of tomorrow.

nine

THE FINAL LINK OF
THE DEMAND CHAIN

"If we do not plan for the future because we live in the
present, we will remain in the past."
—Abraham Lincoln

Whether firms manufacture products, distribute them, or help
develop product brands, all demand-chain partners participate in
the final link of the demand chain—the point at which consumers
buy products. The success of the entire chain ultimately relies on
the performance in the market of the partners that connect with and
sell to consumers. How will demand chains connect with consumers
in the future? The possibilities—or emerging forms of retailing—
will impact not only on the success of the current chain, but the
strategies mind-to-market leaders will adopt in the future.

THE MANY CHANNELS OF RETAIL

Mind-to-market retailers have an arsenal of weapons at their disposal that can make reaching consumers more efficient, effective,
and exciting. Some methods, like electronic retailing, are revolu-
tionary, but most are and will continue to be evolutionary, including

direct marketing through mail and catalogs, direct selling in homes and offices, and direct stores owned and operated by manufacturers.

"Multichannel retailing"—or reaching consumers through a variety of means, including stores, catalogs, direct selling, and electronically—requires a new mind-set for many market leaders. While implementing any one of the following strategies can spell success, the best multichannel retailers will probably use all approaches to sell their wares effectively. These include:

- Store-based retailing

- Direct selling

- Electronic retailing

HYPERMARKETS

While mass retailing has become the retail strategy of choice in the United States, "hypermarkets"—or massive stores featuring groceries, soft and hard goods, with inventory stacked inside the stores on pallets sometimes as high as 32 feet—dominate retail competition in Europe, Africa, Latin America, and some parts of Asia. The acceptance of these hypermarkets, which range in size from 60,000 to 200,000 square feet, in the United States and Canada has been limited to date. (Only a few firms such as Meijer, with a strong regional concentration, have been able to adopt some of the leading features of hypermarkets and make a go of the concept.)

WHERE TO SHOP?

The reality today is that Americans live and shop in an overstored, overmalled, and downright overbuilt retail environment. And it's getting worse. Today, America has over 28,500 shopping centers, compared to just 2,000 in 1957. And we've leapfrogged from 8 square feet of retail space for every living American two decades ago to an average of 20 square feet per person today.

Some industry leaders and analysts look at the retail industry and see successful retailers. Others see failing retailers. I look at the industry and see too many retailers. And too few customers.

Given this reality, one of the most significant questions facing location-based retailers is, Where will consumers want to shop in the future? Just as an increasing number of options exist of how to buy, there are now more places than ever before where shoppers can buy. The possibilities include regional shopping malls, mega-malls, neighborhood strip centers, power strips, value malls (or factory outlets), downtown shopping areas, other people's homes, or the comfort of consumers' own homes. Room exists for some in each category, but not as many of each type as retailers will build or create.

Location strategies will be more important in the future than ever before. Retailers with too few or too many stores often fail, and so do retailers who set up shop on the wrong street, in the wrong shopping center, or in the wrong city. The competitive reality dictates that winning retailers must work as hard to find the best locations as they work to attract consumers from other retailers. Unless of course, they don't depend on retail locations.

GOING RIGHT TO THE CONSUMER

In the first half of this century, direct selling was common. It made sense when women stayed home watching children and keeping house and often had neither the time nor the ability to shop away from home. Though the door-to-door salesman peddling Fuller brushes, Jewell Tea, and *Encyclopaedia Brittanica* may seem like retail relics today, in fact, direct selling that matches consumers' on-the-go lifestyles has staged something of a comeback. Direct sales enable the salesperson to go wherever the consumer wants to buy—home, office, or social setting.

The best direct sellers have developed innovative ways to turn these challenges into opportunities and profits galore. And while direct sellers can call on customers at their convenience, increasingly today companies like Tupperware, Mary Kay, Pampered Chef, and Home Interior employ a party format to reach people. This way, folks have the chance to visit with friends while shopping.

A Basket Case

Dave Longaberger, founder of the Longaberger Company, a Dresden, Ohio–based direct-marketing purveyor of heirloom-quality, handcrafted baskets, was initially frustrated when trying to sell his baskets through local retail channels. His baskets faced fierce competition from cheap imports. However, one person who did buy the baskets wrote asking to buy them wholesale to sell to her friends, thus setting off the proverbial lightbulb in Longaberger's head. He then seized upon this opportunity to create a new supply chain for his baskets.

The Longaberger Company, founded in 1973, grew steadily during the 1970s and 1980s (the Longaberger family had been in the basket business for several generations before this new company was organized). Today the founder's daughters, Tami Longaberger Kaido and Rachel Longaberger Schmidt, are, respectively, president of the company and senior vice president of community affairs.

Party Time!

At basket parties held in homes all over America, customers hear Dave Longaberger's story—how he persevered against hardship, a learning disability, and Appalachian poverty to make and sell baskets woven by local artisans using 100-year-old techniques. Customers then get to examine the handmade, individually signed baskets, which range in price from $25 to $200; some older limited editions now command between several hundred and several thousand dollars as collectors' items. The company now has a sales force of 29,000, with the consultants themselves representing a high proportion of Longaberger's best-customer list. Like Mary Kay salespeople, some Longaberger sales consultants can earn six-figure incomes when they reach the top.

Tami Longaberger Kaido says that direct sales are especially suited for the modern woman (and others) who can work as hard as they want but at their own pace and receive proportionate returns. That's why increasing numbers of entrepreneurs are joining the direct sales force of Longaberger and similar organizations.

Weaving a Better Demand Chain

Direct sales drive the Longaberger demand chain. So does direct marketing. Unlike most manufacturing plants that produce products and then try to sell them, consumers dictate which Longaberger baskets are made and in what quantities. As a result, the company needs less capital to finance raw materials and production than do most manufacturers. Production starts after consumers' orders and payments are received at the factory, eliminating excess materials, inventory, and unnecessary markdowns.

While consumers must wait up to six weeks for orders to arrive, they don't mind. In fact, this waiting period only underscores the quality and care that go into the product. Consultants call when they receive orders, and consumers come pick them up.

Longaberger's unique demand chain benefits from the large number of working mothers longing to belong to a group and earn their own money and from consumers who buy several products several times per year. The firm controls every aspect of manufacturing, wholesaling, logistics, and retailing. The Longaberger story proves that if the existing supply chain doesn't work well, innovative mind-to-market leaders can create their own demand chain.

THE IMPORTANCE OF CATALOGS

Catalogs pack a lot of firepower in the war to win consumer minds. More detailed information is conveyed in the item descriptions in catalog pages than most store personnel generally offer. Indeed, direct marketing—or sending information directly to consumers in the form of catalogs or mail—will continue to grow in importance in the 21st century, due to customers' time famine as well as their growing disenchantment with on-the-hoof shopping as a leisure activity.

Direct marketing has worked for firms such as L.L. Bean, Lillian Vernon, and Peterman, which get the majority, if not all, of their sales from catalogs. In fact, the combined total sales of all current forms of direct marketing amount to about $57 billion, or slightly more than one-half of the total sales of the nation's largest retailer, Wal-Mart.

In true multichannel form, direct marketing also nicely boosts sales for location-based retailers such as Nordstrom, Eddie Bauer, Nieman-Marcus, Williams-Sonoma, and Victoria's Secret, while serving as an advertising tool in promoting the retailer in the mind of consumers. This method aids in developing the store itself as a brand, as in the case of the Victoria's Secret catalog, one of the most widely circulated and probably the best-known catalogs in the world, with over 350 million copies circulated in 1996. The catalog has proven to be a highly effective ongoing marketing tool for the company.

In the future, successful direct marketers will pitch their wares wherever high-income consumers congregate—in airports, resorts, and professional offices. The best catalogs will appear in fine hotel rooms and behind airplane seats, touting tie-in programs with resorts and advertising direct response messages on the CNN airport channel. Partnering with a good distributor like UPS or RPS might make same-day delivery service in many cities possible. Consumers may even be able to order merchandise while in flight and pick it up in the airport when they land.

NEW MEDIA: FROM CD-ROMS TO ELECTRONIC COMMERCE

While most direct marketers still use traditional promotional methods such as mailings, catalogs, and newspaper inserts, retail-sales opportunities are emerging with new media ranging from CD-ROMs to electronic commerce. There's little doubt that these forms of retailing can only increase their share of the retail pie in the future. (In 1997, electronic commerce was estimated to account for between 1 to 3 percent of our total retail pie.) But in order to understand the potential of the technology available to retailers, one must first understand when electronic commerce constitutes the best method to reach consumers.

Selling Cars in Cyberspace

When Peter Ellis pictures the future, he sees cars in cyberspace. He believes in electronic retailing as much as in selling cars, and he's planning to do both in the future. As a car dealer for Chrysler and Ford, he was one of the first to try selling cars to consumers on the QVC home shopping network in the early 1990s. Although that idea did not take off as he'd hoped, the experience did launch him into cyberspace, where he landed on CompuServe and the World Wide Web.

Because there are distinct advantages to purchasing vehicles on-line over buying them off the lot, the idea seems like a winner. For starters, dealers cannot carry every combination of model, color, and accessory package that consumers may desire. (If they did, it would drive prices higher than consumers would be willing to pay. In fact, the high cost of prime real estate and fancy showrooms already hikes costs.) On-line auto shopping gives consumers access to far more selections. What's more, when you're on-line, you don't have to deal with a common consumer complaint— pushy salespeople.

Ellis's Auto-By-Tel service, which reaches an audience of 12,000 or more potential customers per month on the information highway, eliminates most of the hassles from the auto search and purchase process. With Ellis's firm—or one of several others emerging in the cyber-retailing race—customers no longer have to battle traffic driving from dealer to dealer, roam around car lots and glitzy, smoke-filled showrooms comparing features and options on cars, and haggle with salespeople. With electronic retailing, all you do is click in car requirements and preferences and let your mouse do the walking.

Ellis relays orders to a network of 1,200 dealers, which provides delivery and service. Local dealers pay Auto-By-Tel a fee ranging from $200 to $1,500 a month for referrals and deliver cars to customers' homes or offices within a day or two of the order. Although the margins that dealers who market their cars on-line receive are lower than those from traditional retailing (about $600), on-line marketing expense drops from an average of $400 per car with traditional retailing to about $30. From a consumer perspective, a Chevy Malibu of the same specifications bought by computer is the same Chevy Malibu purchased after hours of tedious shopping and dickering with salespeople.

CHANNEL CHANGERS

Technology enthusiasts optimistically predict that electronic retailing will change the industry as we now know it, regardless of product category or industry. But there is a difference between what technology can do and what it *will* do. Ultimately, consumers decide the fate of technological innovations; they'll decide if electronic commerce on the Internet will become a widely accepted innovation like television or a passing fad like CB radio. Sometimes consumers embrace innovations, but often they actively resist them. New technology changes demand chains only if it solves old problems for consumers better than do the existing solutions, as in the case with Auto-By-Tel. Although there'll always be a group that enjoys window shopping, kicking tires, and sparring with salespeople, the benefits of electronic automobile shopping to many consumers far outweigh the drawbacks.

Realistic rather than inflated predictions of the extent to which electronic retailing will take off must consider how well the current retailing system fits consumers' lifestyles. To get a feel for the future, you'll want to analyze:

- The advantages and disadvantages of a particular technology.

- How the technology fits consumers' lifestyles.

- The fit between the technology and the demand chain.

WHO'S ON THE NET?

At the onset of the Internet craze, proponents of the technology were predicting that electronic retailing would grow to 30 or 40 percent of all retailing in the not-so-distant future. But consumer-behavior specialists believe consumers' lifestyles and wants won't make this optimistic prediction true anytime soon. While a wealth of electronic retailing technologies already exist and are being rapidly developed and refined for use in the next century, certain questions remain unanswered: What proportion of consumers will adopt the technology? How many users will purchase what percentage of their total purchases electronically? And, finally, will this diffusion process take 3 to 4 years, or 30 to 40 years?

The bottom line is: To what degree will interactive, electronic retailing replace in-store retailing?

There are powerful reasons to believe in the future ascendancy of electronic retailing based upon the initial acceptance and rapid diffusion of the Internet itself. The Internet began in the early 1980s, mostly used for military information and academic research. Today use of the Internet is exploding. Currently:

1. Nearly 40 percent of American homes have computers, a number expected to increase to 50 percent by 2000, with those homes having a far higher total income than their computerless counterparts.

2. In 1996, the American Internet User Survey reported that 9.5 million Americans, including 1.1 million children—or 3.6 percent of the population—use the Internet.

3. Two-thirds of Net users look for information weekly; about one-quarter searches daily.

4. Net users are well educated, have above-average incomes (about $62,000 in 1996), and are likely to be male.

5. The group that spends lots of time surfing the Net are called "Net nerds." They spend an average of 6.6 hours a week on the Net.

A lot of people with money are hooked up to (and some hooked on) the Internet. But before becoming overly optimistic about electronic retailing prospects, however, consider a few mitigating circumstances.

Even if half of all computer users were equipped and on-line, the proportion of total consumers able or desiring to shop electronically would remain small. Estimates of the number of American users on-line range from 35 million to 45 million. Most surfers visit fewer than 50 Websites from the millions that are available. Mostly, they gather information, pursue hobbies, and chat on-line. This well-educated segment of the population affects sales of some products, but does not account for a high proportion of retail sales, especially products where females are the dominant buyers.

A recent poll of on-line users shows the various activities they pursue:

Use E-mail	75 percent
Get information on hobby or personal interest	64 percent
Get news	52 percent
Get information for work or business	51 percent
Access bulletin board discussions (or news groups)	36 percent

Get sports information	31 percent
Download software	31 percent
Visit chat rooms	25 percent
Monitor stocks, investments	22 percent
Get information about medical/personal problems	15 percent
Participate in celebrity chats	3 percent

The most common reasons for Web usage are as follows:

Browsing	83 percent
Entertainment	57 percent
Work/Business	50 percent
Business research	38 percent
Academic research	34 percent
Shopping	11 percent

Among those who use the Web for shopping, the most commonly purchased items are books, computer software and hardware, tapes and CDs, casual clothing, videos, home electronics, tickets to plays or concerts, and vacations.

ANALYZING THE TECHNOLOGY OF ELECTRONIC COMMERCE

Most of the interest in electronic retailing currently focuses on the Internet, because of the PC's ability to access and handle data interactively and the relatively low cost associated with it. Consumers complain that logging on and downloading graphics takes too long and is frustrating, thus preventing them from using it. Innovations like cable modems, which would have the ability to speed the process, could stimulate usage of electronic retailing. However, additional usage could slow down the system dramatically—at least before the kinks are worked out.

Technology that transmits information is easier to develop than technology that transmits the products consumers buy. With conventional retailing, customers walk out of the store with the product in hand. They don't deal with the problems and costs of delivery that accompany electronic retailing.

Home delivery will inhibit the widespread adoption of electronic retailing into areas that are being tested today like on-line grocery shopping. Among higher-income households most likely to purchase groceries electronically, generally no one is home during the day to take delivery.

But a few solutions to the delivery problem exist. First, a computerized distribution system could establish delivery "windows," or periods during which the customer agrees to be home to take delivery. A complex system of scheduling trucks, drivers, and delivery routes is entirely possible, though costly.

Another alternative solution is 24-hour consumer distribution points where consumers could pick up electronically purchased goods at convenient locations. A firm such as Kinko's, which is already open 24 hours and has postal boxes, could do the trick. Another option is for consumers to construct individual safe boxes housed on porches or beside driveways, garages, or gates that delivery personnel could access.

It's not hard to predict how technologies will be either adopted or rejected by consumers and supply chains, and the rate at which they'll "diffuse," or be accepted. A set of principles used for such analysis originally appeared in Everett Rogers's classic book, *The Diffusion of Innovations*, providing a framework for analyzing how quickly electronic commerce will be accepted. Whether or not electronic retailing will become a major force in retail sales will be determined by the factors listed in Figure 9.1.

Relative Advantage

To succeed, consumers must believe electronic retailing offers a relative advantage over the current setup, that electronic retailing can solve their problems better than existing channels. If consumers are casting about for alternatives, it means that they're dissatisfied with existing forms of retailing, whether they be retail stores, catalogs, or direct selling.

What's more, these consumers must have the tools needed to shop electronically—namely, a computer and modem as well as access to on-line services—and the motivation and know-how to use the ser-

Figure 9.1   Business to Business:
Helping Solve Your Customers' Customers Problems

Consumer Trend: _____

Customer Name	Industry	How Will Industry Be Affected?	How Will Company Be Affected?	How Will Their Customers/ Consumers Be Affected?	What New Problems in the Market-place Can We Help Them Solve?	What Solutions Can We Offer?	Who and Which Channel Members Can Assist?

vice. The group of people fitting this bill still represents just a tiny fraction of the population. And of this group, a smaller proportion is female, who constitute most retail shoppers in the United States.

When considering electronic shopping, consumers have concerns about the process that might inhibit exploring this venue. These might include worries about how long will it take to boot a computer and go through numerous menus, commands, and icons to find a product and buy it. Some might wonder if shopping the Net is as convenient as shopping in a catalog or a store that generally carries a large selection of items. Will the item that's displayed on the computer monitor or TV screen be true to the color and styling when they take delivery? Another concern might be: Will I have hassles with exchanges or refunds?

While providing some basis for comparison with on-line retailing, catalog shopping offers a number of obvious advantages over its computerized cousin. Catalog customers can "shop" in bathrooms, bathtubs, and on airplanes with ease; they can scan pages in a matter of seconds—a fraction of the time it takes to find a Website and download graphics. Catalogs allow people to do other things while shopping, such as visit with family, eat a meal, or watch TV. One thing that catalogs cannot provide, however, is models coming to life on videotape, demonstrating products.

Consumer Compatibility

How compatible is electronic commerce with the behaviors and lifestyles of the mass market? At present, the majority of consumers don't have computers at home (though that could change). Fewer women than men use computers at home, in part because women are more likely to use them at work and don't want to face the glare of a computer in their spare time.

Net nerds are most likely to find electronic commerce compatible with their lifestyles, and they will buy a lot of things electronically. And computer-literate consumers accustomed to buying stocks, banking services, and other products via telephone will make the transition more readily to electronic commerce than others. But unless a great relative advantage or degree of compatibility exists, don't expect a rapid movement to electronic commerce by most consumers when buying most products.

Complexity

The more complex the new product, the more difficult it is to gain acceptance. Microwave ovens diffused rapidly through mainstream America because they were easy to use. Electronic shopping will appeal to a mass audience only when a minicomputer or setbox on top of the TV is no more complex and time-consuming to operate than a remote control.

Trialability

When consumers can experiment with or try a new technology, they're more likely to adopt the product. CompuServe, Prodigy, AOL, and other services, for example, provide free software usually accompanied by a month's free trial to those wanting to venture on-line. Even though they're free and easy to use, most consumers discard those discs without ever trying them. Electronic retailers can try to attract consumers with free usage and discounted merchandise, iron-clad guarantees, no-hassle return procedures, and sampling of the electronic shopping service in stores or other public places. But be forewarned that these methods are no guarantee for success. Consumer resistance may be greater than you would expect.

Observability

Before they buy, most consumers have to be shown new technologies, preferably by a neighbor or friend. When room air conditioners were introduced in the 1950s, adoption occurred mostly within concentrated areas where neighbors observed neighbors living in cool comfort and often tried it out for themselves. Being able to observe before purchasing reduces consumers' anxieties about new technologies and purchases. Because of its one-on-one setup, electronic retailing is at a relative disadvantage when it comes to observability. However, if the platform for the Internet were to transfer to cable TV with large-screen display and more conspicuous observability, product diffusion would accelerate.

MESHING TECHNOLOGY WITH THE SUPPLY CHAIN

From the perspective of logistics and supply-chain management, electronic commerce cuts some costs and hikes others. Shifting retailing away from expensive shopping centers decreases overhead costs. But electronic retailing increases some costs by shifting functions such as assembly and delivery from consumers (who perform them for free) to paid employees. Companies already involved in direct marketing have a real advantage when shifting into electronic sales because they've already solved some distribution problems that new electronic retailers will have to tackle.

Certain types of product lines are more likely to succeed with electronic commerce from the perspective of the consumer as well as the supply chain. They possess the following characteristics:

Business Attributes for Success with Electronic Retailing

1. High inventory costs that can be reduced by centralized retailing.

2. Efficient physical distribution exists or can be achieved.

3. Database management that allows focus on core segment strategies.

4. Technology that is simple to use, reliable, and lower cost than traditional retailing channels.

5. Investment in branding or standards to achieve consumer confidence in product quality.

6. Direct marketing supply chain exists and functions efficiently.

7. Existing retailers have high costs of labor or physical facilities that need not be duplicated with electronic retailing.

8. Suppliers, manufacturers, and retailers are all committed to electronic commerce.

Consumer Attributes for Success with Electronic Retailing

1. The purchase is infrequent.

2. Frequent need exists to find more information on product and/or current method of obtaining information is difficult or troublesome.

3. Out-of-area search is required.

4. A highly standardized product or a unique, one-of-a-kind product is sought.

5. Specific product features are known.

6. Standards for comparing or guaranteeing quality (such as brands or certification organizations) are readily available.

7. Inadequate selection available from existing channels.

8. Consumers are physically unable to shop or leave home.

SEARCHING FOR THE RIGHT FIT

In the future, a combination of electronic retailing and in-store retailing might best fit consumers' needs, at least initially. Electronic retailing fits parts of the business-to-business market well. For companies that order reams of paper, envelopes by the thousands, and paper clips by the case, computer-based ordering and flexible delivery times work well. It's a good forum for a company that buys new heavy industrial equipment and wants to sell existing equipment. Since many businesses are on the Internet already, it makes sense that potential buyers are on-line as well. Going-out-of-business sales or liquidations also fit the parameters of electronic retailing. The liquidation of filing cabinets, paper products, computer equipment, and even heavy equipment can be described on-line, reaching an appropriate audience.

Perhaps the best "Net fit" for most consumers is the product-search stage. For instance, people can scan the Net for real-estate offerings locally or at points distant, search for product comparisons between manufacturers, and compare prices and product availability. Such possibilities are numerous. Consumers may use the Net for their search, and buy from a local retailer if they choose. The Internet is a great marketing tool and means of getting information to customers and employees. The best mind-to-market leaders will use Websites to communicate with consumers who browse the Net for information, including the name and location of the nearest retailer carrying the desired product.

Winners in electronic retailing are concentrated among very specific product lines, brands, and core market segments. In addition to vehicles, a number of product categories make obvious fits for electronic retailing.

AND THE WINNERS ARE . . .

- *Financial products* such as common stocks are logical candidates to be purchased through electronic retailing. Knowledgeable consumers can obtain information about the current price of 100 shares of AT&T more quickly on-line than by calling a broker. From the supply side, Charles Schwab can dispense information and conduct transactions through electronic channels more efficiently than competitors who must pay a staff to sit in offices and answer calls. From the consumer's standpoint, paying commissions for routine transactions makes little sense when other buying options exist, unless the broker adds value through knowledge.

  I predict that a large proportion of retail stock brokerage and similar transactions will take place electronically by the years 2010 to 2020. This transition is well under way. Already, fully 23 percent of Charles Schwab's sales come through the Internet. Gearing up for this inevitability, the National Association of Securities Dealers has dedicated $40 million to revamp its entire computer system to put data about its 500,000 registered brokers on the Internet. Consumers still wanting to deal with a human being will soon be able to check out his or her credentials on the Internet!

- *Virtual bookstores* providing a direct pipeline to nearly every title from nearly every publisher, all from the comfort and convenience of the nearest computer. The winner to date, not only of all on-line bookstores but of Internet commerce generally, is Amazon.com. The company operates from a jumbled storeroom in Seattle backed by a humming box of computers running its Website to distant parts of the globe. Led by former stock analyst Jeff Bezos, since starting with zero sales in 1995, Amazon has been doubling nearly every quarter, achieving 1996 sales of $16 million and an initial stock offering that brought a buying frenzy when it was first offered to the public in May of 1997. Amazon is a river of information about how to succeed on the Internet by offering more than the opportunity to buy a selection from its 2.5 million titles as the self-decribed "Earth's Biggest Bookstore," but it has yet to make a profit. Amazon also provides book reviews, service, and an opportunity to join the global village of book enthusiasts. On-line customers not only read information about books written by Amazon's experts, they are encouraged to write their own reviews and leave them for other interested viewers. When customers leave this information, along with their history of book buying, Amazon has a valuable data warehouse about its best customers with which it may send them an E-mail message when a book is published that might strike a customer's lifestyle and interests. Amazon also proves the power of demand chain transportation with its methods of supplying books. While Amazon's virtual bookstore advertises the availability of 2.5 million books, it only stocks about 400 of the top-selling titles. The rest are outsourced from nearby Ingram, one of America's largest book wholesalers. The more obscure books are shipped direct from the publishers. Combining information from consumers, alliances with other supply-chain members, and computer linkages throughout the demand chain is a formula for successful selling—one that Barnes and Noble and other booksellers are quickly emulating. It is a formula likely to be repeated for music CDs and other products with similar demand and supply characteristics.

- *Travel agencies* writing routine tickets for business clients can expect to be replaced with on-line electronic ticketing in the near future. Already American Airlines provides over 450 pages on its World Wide Web site (htp://www.amrcorp.com/AA). It recently unveiled Aaccess, a comprehensive combination of technology products and airport enhancements that leapfrogs current ticketless travel and automated boarding. American's goal is to be the first to provide the technology needed to organize and carry out the entire travel process for individual consumers from booking to takeoff.

  The SABRE Group, the world leader in the electronic distribution of information technology for the travel industry, provides solutions for the airline industry. In 1996, travel agencies with more than 29,000 locations in more than 70 countries subscribed to SABRE, and more than 2.5 million individuals subscribed to Travelocity and easySABRE, the company's consumer-direct products. American offers its AAdvantage frequent fliers Travelocity to check their accounts as well as make reservations and purchase tickets on American and other airlines. Travelocity (http://www.travelocity.com) offers do-it-yourself travelers access to information and tickets for shows, shopping, special events, and other attractions on a worldwide basis.

- *Electronic art retailers* can offer substantial advantages to consumers compared to the existing supply chain of gallery-based art dealers. Under the current system, if a collector wants to buy a Lichtenstein, Miró, or Rembrandt, he or she must first visit galleries and view—if they're lucky—a few paintings by each artist at each location. Just as no car dealer can have every possible configuration of vehicle, no gallery can afford to carry the complete works of any famous artist due to the high cost of holding slow-moving inventory. Most customers would like to see a large selection before making this infrequent and expensive purchase. The existing distribution system fails to provide consumers that opportunity.

Dealers, however, already have computerized networks enabling them to scan the globe to find available art. They also have the mechanisms to certify authenticity and arrange safe shipping. Today dealers use this network and ordinarily receive a markup of 50 percent on selling price.

It won't take long before knowledgeable customers plug into the network, bypassing the retail art gallery completely. Tim Warner, president of Artists Online (http://www.onlineart.com), points out that the experience of visiting one art gallery can now be extended to visiting many galleries worldwide in the same day via electronic shopping. One entrepreneur already offering retail customers such a service over the Web is Pierette Van Cleve, president of Art Cellar Exchange in San Diego (http://www.artcellarex.com). The only serious drawback of pursuing art electronically today is that downloading takes time, and the final image on many computer screens often falls short of expectations. However, as technologies improve, both of these problems should quickly vanish. For the serious art shopper, the financial advantages of shopping electronically (as well as having the ability to control and expedite the search process) far outweigh the downsides of this search method.

ON-LINE RETAILING: THE FUTURE

Each business should evaluate the opportunities the Internet and other forms of electronic retailing can provide. Though clearly some retail categories mesh well with electronic retailing, others may be a stretch. In the next two to three decades, it seems safe to evaluate electronic retailing in the context of the following propositions:

- Electronic retailing will increase rapidly but remain a small percentage of the total retail pie.

- Electronic retailing will be important for specific product lines, but not all of them.

- Electronic retailing will be important as an information and communication tool for many mind-to-market retailers.

- Electronic retailing will supply information to retailers and the entire demand chain about consumers' wants, problems, and preferences, if two-way communication is set up by the retailer.

In my view, statistical growth, in terms of "hits" on various Websites, may be high, but market share in terms of retail sales will be relatively low. Even if electronic retailing does capture as much as 10 to 20 percent of total retail sales in the next two to three decades, in-store, location-based retailing will continue to hold the safety net beneath the tightrope of on-line retailing. As with all demand chains, consumers will ultimately determine how successful on-line retailing becomes, voting daily with their pocketbooks, time, and attention.

REACHING CONSUMERS WITH SMART HOMES

The race to create so-called smart homes has begun and is attracting into the fray some of the heaviest hitters in the world of business. A "smart home" links communications, energy, entertainment, retailing, and security with the information needed to increase the efficiency of all of these arenas. In the past, each home received each product or service from a different supplier. In the digital age of tomorrow, however, the smart home will look more like the diagram in Figure 9.2.

It would make sense that the company that has electronic access to the home of the consumer would hold significant power over hundreds of members in a myriad of demand chains. Bill Gates has

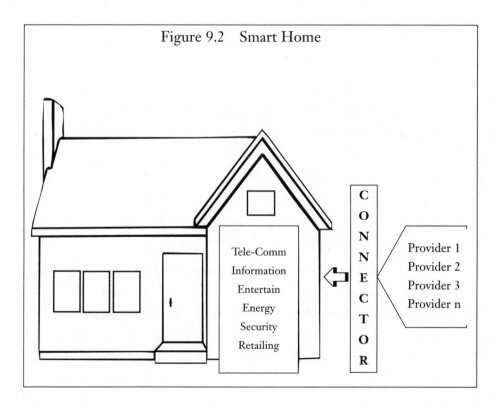

Figure 9.2   Smart Home

already figured this out, and Microsoft is vying for the job of CEO of smart homes around the world. At the same time, individual gas, electric, telecommunications, cable, and computer companies that already have access to homes are eager to increase their power and value in the market. The ultimate supplier to the smart home will increase its value to the entire demand chain because of its access to consumers.

AT&T, TCI, and TVA are colossal organizations—the largest in their respective fields of telephony, cable communications, and electrical-energy generation. All three formerly regulated monopolies (and now rapidly deregulating companies) are in hand-to-hand, survival-of-the-fittest combat for access to consumers' homes—and minds—in the 21st century. All three are positioning themselves to be major players in the coming smart-home market.

Smart homes may get their entertainment from Disney/ABC, their telephony from a variety of providers (ranging from AT&T or British Telecom to TCI or Warner), their computerized databases from CompuServe, AOL, or the Internet, their energy from a power company anyplace in the world, and their interactive shopping from companies ranging from Nordstrom and Wal-Mart to small independent retailers worldwide connected to the Web. Consumers and businesses need all of these products and services, but they don't need a separate connection for each one. In fact, one connection to the rest of the world would be ideal for both consumer and provider.

But the question is: Who will provide the hookup from the smart homes to the rest of the world? And whom will consumers trust to be their primary interface with the world—their energy company, telephone company, or cable company? Or perhaps Bill Gates?

Visionary leaders, not just technology, will determine the best consumer connection. The organization that provides basic access to the smart homes of the future will be in the driver's seat. Channel commanders may not own the other providers, but they will be positioned to command the channels of distribution for communications, information, entertainment, security, and energy—all products likely to offer some of the greatest growth and profits in the future.

Enron

Enron may soon be coming to a home near you. In the rapidly deregulating world of energy production, transmission, and marketing, Enron is rapidly becoming a household name. One of the world's largest integrated natural gas companies, it holds approximately $13 billion in assets and also functions as one of the largest independent developers and producers of electricity. At its headquarters in Houston, the company recently announced its vision of $1 billion net income by the year 2000, approximately double its 1995 net income. Given its track record, this would seem to be a realizable goal. From 1988 to 1995, Enron's total return to shareholders shot up 369 percent compared to a 65 percent increase among its competitive peers. Power marketers who want to survive utility deregulation and grab a piece of the retail pie must convince customers why they should buy their electrons instead of their competitors'.

As the energy industry undergoes deregulation, energy as a commodity has reached puberty and is transforming itself into a value-added, image-conscious, competitively positioned product. Enron and its competitors have entered the marketing zone, where each will be forced to understand, relate to, and communicate with consumers.

Enron and the others are all vying for the job of consumer connection to the supply chain through the smart home. The coordinator of all roads entering into consumers' homes will be the gatekeeper to consumers' minds, needs, and pocketbooks. The smart-home supplier will be able to collect information from consumers and pass products to them, serving as the connection between the end and beginning the demand-chain process.

One of the company's most innovative programs gives free electricity to Enron customers. The Enron Energy Rewards Program lets customers earn free electricity for every unit of Enron natural gas used. Most of Enron's marketing programs in the past targeted business customers. But, with this new program, Enron set its sights on residential markets where it'll be possible to buy gas or electricity as easily as selecting MCI or Sprint for long-distance telephone service.

When the smart homes of the future get powered up for the needs of information, entertainment, shopping, and energy management, Enron's pitch, however, is direct: "World's Leading Energy Company—creating energy solutions worldwide for a better environment."

Enron's bundling of electricity and gas creates a pattern for the future. CompuServe and AOL charge for their information services, but AT&T gives them away to get access to telecommunication consumers. The World Wide Web also provides free information, using telephone lines or cable provided by other firms who are mystified about how to charge for such usage. When cable companies provide telephony, as they have announced they'll do, how much will they provide free in order to be a consumer's primary entertainment provider? Cable firms and power companies are united in their need for ditches in which to run lines to access consumers' homes; in such a case, alliances between these types of entities is virtually predestined.

Through the doors of these smart homes, the stage is set for both competition and cooperation among all energy, telecommunications, cable, security, and technology firms. In the future, there'll be a host of strategic alliances between global giants, the inevitable wave of multibillion-dollar mergers and acquisitions, along with a bundling of goods and services along new demand chains.

FROM MIND TO MARKET AND BEYOND

The final stage in the mind-to-market process—the delivery of goods to consumers—is also the beginning point of a new mind-to-market cycle. The point at which consumers purchase products, whether from traditional location-based retailers, direct sales networks, or electronically, provides a great opportunity for companies to connect with consumers. Information about how pleased consumers are with the products they purchase is only one piece of information the demand chain needs in order to improve itself. Mind-to-market leaders need to probe consumers' satisfaction levels with the store (or buying method) as well. Four potential outcomes can result:

- Satisfaction with the product and satisfaction with the store.

- Satisfaction with the product and dissatisfaction with the store.

- Dissatisfaction with the product and satisfaction with the store.

- Dissatisfaction with the product and dissatisfaction with the store.

When customers leave the store happy with their experience inside the store and happy with their purchase, they're likely to return. Obviously, this is the outcome for which most retailers strive. Similarly, bad shopping conditions inside the store coupled with poor products quickly lead to bankruptcy. When consumers experience satisfaction on one level and dissatisfaction at the other, interesting, momentum-shifting retail dynamics arise.

The first few times consumers purchase products with which they're unhappy, they may still return to the store (for the reasons they chose it originally) and simply switch brands. But if such experiences occur across multiple product categories, consumers experience dissatisfaction and relate it not only to the products and brands but to the retailer as well. Over time, product dissatisfaction leads to store and buying-process dissatisfaction, causing consumers to no longer trust the store to offer quality products they can rely on. When the store does a poor job as purchasing agent for the customer, he or she will find a retailer that offers brands and products they can trust.

However, in today's hypercompetitive retail environment, just having the products and brands people want to buy is not enough to make for an entirely satisfactory experience. Retailers ranging from traditional department stores to off-price, closeout stores can no longer rely on the pull of national brands and availability of product assortment to secure customers for the long term. With so many choices available, all retailers today must deliver on the details that consumers deem most important to make their shopping experiences pleasant, if not pleasurable. These "details" may include clean, well-lit stores, spotless rest rooms, wide shopping aisles, quick checkout, and accommodating service.

THE FOUNDATION OF MIND-TO-MARKET LEADERSHIP

Getting the details right is an inevitable outcome of becoming a mind-to-market leader. Getting there is not a product, but rather a process driven by consumers. It is achieved by:

- Gathering and analyzing knowledge about consumers, especially their problems and unmet needs.

- Identifying a group of organizations to perform the functions needed in the demand chain.

- Sharing knowledge about consumers with demand-chain members.

- Developing products and services that solve customers' problems in conjunction with other firms in the demand chain.

- Shifting the functions that need to be performed by the demand chain to the organizations that can perform them most effectively and cost efficiently.

- Developing the best logistics, transportation, and distribution methods to deliver products and services to consumers in the marketplace.

Mind-to-market leaders serve as the masters of the demand chain that links the desires in consumers' minds to products or services in the marketplace. Sometimes these leaders are individual companies. Sometimes they're nonlinear, boundary-spanning organizations as is the case with Nike, which defies categorization as a retailer, wholesaler, or manufacturer. Each organization crosses over traditional operating boundaries and performs the functions they are best able to complete. The process ends with execution in the marketplace. Demand chains begin and end in the same place—with the consumer.

In a world where time and talent have become two of our most precious resources, the best companies must organize supply chains to get their products from the mind of consumers to the market in less time, with fewer people than ever before and well ahead of the competition. Too much supply and too little demand destroys a supply chain and crushes many of its members; too little supply and too much demand for unmet needs drives customers to competitors.

Winners recognize changes in demand from consumers and customers and change both themselves and the supply chain, while traditional firms settle for what the market gives them.

CHOOSING THE RIGHT DEMAND-CHAIN PARTNERS

Throughout this book, you've read about mind-to-market leaders and many demand-chain members that are responsible, at least in part, for the success of the entire chain. But choosing the best demand-chain partners for long-term market dominance challenges firms of all sizes. Sometimes demand chains are formed based on the reputations of the members. Sometimes they arise from existing relationships.

The firms that hope to survive the courting stage of the relationship must look for something beyond the reputation, resources, and financial statements of potential partners. Money and love often prove insufficient to sustain a marriage between two people; there needs to be trust and honesty as well. The same holds true for demand-chain partners.

Manco and Applied Industrial Technologies are two intermediary companies in the demand chain that operate in an open environment, sharing information—sometimes strategic in nature—with their vendors and customers. Such open dialogue could not exist without complete trust among demand-chain members.

What fosters trust among demand-chain members? Increasingly, it's similar values that represent what the company stands for in terms of how it treats its employees, customers, partners, and communities. With trust, demand-chain partners can work closely together, sharing ideas, information, hopes, fears, disappointments, and successes.

Applied believes strongly in the power of values in the demand chain. Often acquiring firms to build its demand chain, company executives evaluate firms on a variety of traditional criteria, including profitability and financial ratios. But they also take a hard look at the value systems of companies. In a recent acquisition evaluation, Applied's Jack Dannemiller terminated negotiations with a prospect company that was highly profitable when he and others realized that they weren't getting honest responses. That called the company's value system into question. "Values before short-term profits" is fast becoming the motto of many great companies like ServiceMaster, Worthington Foods, and Newell, which believe that trust among demand-chain members serves as the foundation of great mind-to-market chains.

IN THE PALM OF YOUR HAND

So, you've reached the end of this book and may be wondering, "What about the hand on the cover?" You've surmised that everything in life has meaning, a significance that perhaps is not understood at first glance. Well, you're right; this hand does have meaning.

Doubtless, you noticed the UPC code stamped on the palm of this consumer. It represents the possibility of the ultimate method to record and track consumer transaction data. Would it be possible to embed a small computer chip in every person's hand or tattoo a unique code on the palm to be scanned when consumers check out of stores? All items would automatically be tallied and applied to that person's credit card or bank account as identified by the UPC code, without a physical transaction of money for goods. Retailers and manufacturers would be able to profile specific consumers' brand preferences and product choices, track who's buying what, and virtually eliminate the transaction that occurs in the front of the store. If this chip idea seems too far-fetched, perhaps some combination scanner and fingerprint identification system could work in its stead.

But the juxtaposition of this futuristic technology with the humanistic hand underscores the point that marketers should never just analyze the numbers. I'm certainly not advocating thinking of consumers as dehumanized numbers—in fact, just the opposite is true. In an age of computers and scanners, marketers are exploring new ways to get the type of information discussed in this book to drive their demand chains. But remember these are numbers. They should always be accompanied by sensitivity to the emotions, fears, and urges that make us human. The best market researchers have the talent of being able to look at data and put them together with some intangible human insight and see what other people do not see.

WHAT WILL THE HISTORY BOOKS SAY?

I often wonder what the business history books of the year 2050 will say about the coming turn of the century. Perhaps the greatest understatement historians will make is that it was an era of change. While change is nothing new, the rate of change is what has and will continue to set corporate minds of the world racing. We have watched as change evolved from gradual to rapid to turbocharged. The business scholars of tomorrow will study the companies of today that survived and thrived by adapting to changes in their environments and to changes dictated by their customers. They will also study the thousands of firms that will have reached extinction because of their failure to adapt.

Consumer research can lead to the strategic-level changes needed throughout an organization or supply chain to adapt to changes in the market. But many firms do the research and stop there. The data that research yields must be analyzed, which transforms them into usable information. Then, when information is studied and integrated with other data about the marketplace—gathered in ways described in this book—it becomes knowledge. And, finally, when knowledge is applied according to corporate values and missions and shared with other channel members, it becomes strategy. That is how mind-to-market leaders use knowledge about consumers to formulate initiatives in the market.

The never-ending quest for formulating new mind-to-market strategies comes from the need to change—a never-ending challenge facing firms of all sizes. While hosts of companies around the world fear change because they don't understand the future, mind-to-market leaders—armed with the knowledge and with compatible demand-chain partners to push the envelope of business excellence to the next level—embrace it.

In that embrace lies their salvation and their route to success.

INDEX

About the Author

ROGER D. BLACKWELL is a professor of marketing at the Ohio State University and president of Blackwell Associates, Inc., a consulting firm through which he has worked with many of America's most successful companies.

Roger was cited by the *New York Times* in 1995 as one of the top speakers on the lecture circuit and heralded as a marketing and retail "guru" with the ability to mesmerize his audiences. Having lectured around the world, he is often quoted in such publications as *Business Week, USA Today, Forbes,* and the *Wall Street Journal* and has appeared on numerous television programs including *CBS This Morning.*

He was named "Outstanding Marketing Educator in America" by Sales and Marketing Executives International and "Marketer of the Year" by the American Marketing Association. He also received the "Alumni Distinguished Teaching Award," the highest award given by Ohio State. After thirty years at the university, his depth of knowledge and enthusiasm still make him a favorite among students; he received two teaching awards in 1997 alone.

Roger Blackwell is considered to be one of the founding fathers of consumer behavior as coauthor of one of the leading books in this field, *Contemporary Cases in Consumer Behavior.* It is used by business schools throughout North America, Europe, Asia, and Africa. He has also written twenty-one other books on marketing strategy and research.

Roger received his B.S. and M.S. degrees from the University of Missouri and his Ph.D. from Northwestern University. He also received an honorary doctorate degree from the Cincinnati College of Mortuary Science. He resides in Columbus, Ohio, and serves on numerous boards of both privately and publicly held corporations.